D0029229

THAT'S MENTAL

Turner Publishing Company
Nashville, Tennessee
www.turnerpublishing.com

That's Mental
Copyright © 2019 TKTKTK
All rights reserved

This book or any part thereof may not be reproduced or transmitted in any form or by any means,
electronic or mechanical, including photocopying, recording, or by any information storage and
retrieval system, without permission in writing from the publisher.

This is a work of fiction. All the characters and events portrayed in this book
are either products of the author's imagination or are used fictitiously.

Cover design: TKTKTK
Book design: Karen Sheets de Gracia

Library of Congress Cataloging-in-Publication Data TKTKTK

TKTKTK Hardcover
TKTKTK Paperback
TKTKTK eBook

Printed in the United States of America

19 20 21 22   10 9 8 7 6 5 4 3 2 1

THAT'S
MENTAL

PAINFULLY FUNNY THINGS
THAT DRIVE ME CRAZY
ABOUT BEING MENTALLY ILL

Amanda Rosenberg

TURNER
PUBLISHING COMPANY

dedication TK

CONTENTS

Part 5: Relationships

Part 6: Not Ok but Ok

Appendix

I'M NOT GOOD AT BEING MENTAL

I'm not good at being mental, but I should be.

I've been mentally ill for most of my life and although I've only been aware of it until relatively recently, I've still managed to clock in way over ten thousand hours of solid mental illness time. Which should make me an expert, no, better than an expert. I should be the final boss of depression. I should be tenured in anxiety. I should have an EGOT in trauma which yes, already has its own acronym, but we all know it's not as glamorous!

See? Not good.

I thought mental illness should look a certain way, should feel a certain way, and should taste a certain—not really, but how gross would that be though? I believed there was an official mental illness style bible which housed strict definitions on how certain illnesses presented themselves. Of course, all of these definitions were informed by movies, television, and the news, so instead of a nuanced look at mental disorders, it was simply, "oh, they're just fucking crazy". This is how I understood people with mental illnesses and for many of my formative years, I prided myself on not being one of them, one of *those* people, the ones with the *issues*.

You can't see me, but I am laughing heartily, because I am extremely one of those people. Certified Fresh 100% mental. It took me a long time to recognize it, an even longer time to accept it, and I will spend the rest of my time managing it. But please don't hold out for a happy ending. I didn't go for a jog, drink a green juice, and yoga my way out of a mental disorder. Not that there's anything wrong with that, but there's also nothing right about it either.

Sorry. Not good.

Mental illness is not a competition. People experience mental illness in a myriad of different ways. Just because someone's depression doesn't look or sound like yours doesn't make theirs any less valid. You'll find that there will be things in this book you can relate to and others where you'll be like, "that's never happened to me!" And you want to know why? BECAUSE I WIN AT MENTAL ILLNESS. ALL DAY, BABY.

Bad. Very bad.

I will not inspire you. I will not give you advice and if I do, it'll be mediocre at best. Pretty sure I don't need to state the next part but just to be safe, I am not a mental health professional. I'm just a mental health nobody with a lifetime's worth of experience fighting against a mind that wants her dead.

I feel like you're going to need more specifics other than "fighting against a mind" which I both respect and understand.

I have bipolar II. "There's two?" Yes, there's two. But you're probably more aware of bipolar I. Some people just call it "bipolar" like, what are you too good for a number now? I'm joking, but seriously, put the one back, nobody likes a showboater. I could go into detail about the differences between both, but I'll let you research that online later after you've written a glowing review of this book. Broadly speaking, both bipolars are mood disorders, bipolar I is characterized by extreme manic episodes that can last for at least a week, often more. Bipolar I depressive episodes can last for a couple of weeks. Bipolar II is a mix of both depressive and hypomanic episodes. The hypomanic episodes are intense but usually don't require hospitalization like bipolar I. So yeah, there's two, which means before you shoot off a lazy joke about the weather being "so bipolar lately" I'M GONNA NEED YOU TO SPECIFY ONE OR TWO. I also have a few other mental disorders, but I'll leave you to find them in the book, it'll be like a fun Easter Egg Hunt only the eggs are rotten and it's not fun at all!

Better.

After my psychotic breakdown / suicide attempt / subsequent bipolar II diagnosis, I read a ton of mental illness books, which were harrowing and important, but also harrowing. And while I was grateful to those book for teaching and scaring me, I still had so many unimportant, silly person questions about living with mental illness like "how long is too long without a shower?, and, "is it like a week?", and "am I my therapist's favorite patient? Because I feel like I do have the best stories."

I remember during one of my hospital stints, I managed to make a fellow patient laugh. We were talking about how hard it is to shower when you're depressed. I did a whole bit on being scared of washing my hair because it would require a modicum of effort, instead of kneeling down, crying, and hoping my tears would serve as an adequate conditioner. Because when you're depressed and in the shower, you don't want to be clean, you want to die. Anyway, the joke landed, but you kinda had to be there—and severely depressed—to get it. We laughed. But I felt weird. This was at a time before the proliferation of depression memes, so joking about dying when we'd both attempted suicide felt less droll and more "shit, can we say that?" Like, was this even allowed? Would I be kicked out of mental illness club? At that moment, we didn't care; all that mattered was the sense of relief.

The most fun I had in a psychiatric hospital (yes, there were fun times) was when we talked about people "on the outside." We'd talk about other people's reactions to mental illness, the assumptions they make, and how they want to save us with their crystals. I learned that laughing about being mental was not a crime punishable by death—or in our case, life—but was, in fact, a release. As the old saying goes, laughter is the best medicine (in addition to other lifesaving medications). It's one thing laughing about about "outsiders" with other mentally ill people in a hospital; it's another trying to laugh about it at Linda's dinner party where you don't know anyone. They won't laugh with you. They'll smile and nod and sweep shit under the rug. Well, guess what, Linda? I'm lifting up the rug and taking that shit out! Yes, I'll put it in the bin, I know green is for com- fucking hell Linda, I was making a POINT.

Not bad.

Mental illness is complex and harrowing and inspiring and heartbreaking, but it's also funny and boring and gross and smelly. The flashy, dramatic aspects of mental illness tend to get more airtime than the mundane. It's understandable but also unfair. People will never understand mental illness if you don't give them the full picture. I submit this book for the boring, gross, funny portion of the picture…and heartbreak and a bit of harrow. It's mental illness! Whaddya gonna do? I love to be the one to break it to you but, EVERYONE IS MENTAL. Literally everyone has a mental issue. We should all be afraid of people who think they're mentally well. I'm half joking!

We have to laugh. Because If we don't laugh, we'll die.

Good.

PART 1
BC (Before Crazy)

How I Felt about Mental Illness before I Went Mental

Before I had a mental breakdown, lost my entire mind, got committed to a psych ward, got misdiagnosed with borderline personality disorder, and was sent to rehab—where I was properly diagnosed with bipolar II—I had some choice thoughts about mental illness, and HOO BOY were they problematic.

I believed every stereotype, myth, and rumor. If you'd told me that people with mental illnesses were bred in a lab by aliens as an experiment to test the human race's capacity for empathy, I would have believed it—maybe not the empathy part, but everything else, sure. The point is, I believed everything I'd heard about mental illness without question.

I was never *taught* to be scared of mental illness; I just knew I should be. I had this eerie natural instinct, like how cats just know to shit in that box in your bathroom. I knew that mental people were terrifying. Nobody sat me down and told me about the birds and the bees and the crazies. I learned on the job, like you do with baking or sex.

I never *learned* about the stigma. I absorbed it slowly over time through some sort of societal osmosis. It came from everywhere: a kid on the playground twirling their finger next to their temple and calling you "cuckoo," straitjackets worn as Halloween costumes, an abrupt change in the weather from sunny to rainy being called "schizo." The nineties were a real hoot!

In my mind, these were nothing more than harmless gestures and silly sayings. If the term *loony bin* didn't have its roots in asylums where the crazy, the poor, and the not-crazy were tormented day in and day out, I'd think it was quite a playful little phrase. *Loony bin*, like a cartoon trash can or the name of a Scandinavian woodwind instrument. "We have Greg on the piccolo, Denise on the alto clarinet, and Pat on the loony bin. Thank you so much for coming out. We've been the Good Woods, good night!"

To be clear, I'm not trying to change the way the world talks about mental illness with this one chapter—although if it does happen, let the record show it was all because of me and this chapter. I'm in no way qualified to go around trying to change people's hearts and minds, especially since I still use the word *crazy* but only to describe myself, or in response to people's boring ass stories "you saw Diane in CVS? That's crazy". Using the appropriate language is important and I'm trying to do better. But I also called this book *That's Mental*. So, you know, there's that.

I know that these problematic feelings aren't new or groundbreaking, and I'm certain most of you reading this book have had similar thoughts. For those of you shaking your head like "I've never had a disparaging thought about mental illness in my entire life, but this is an excellent book," then may I suggest you climb down from that comically high horse of yours and join us in the gutter because you're a lying swine! But I'm so glad you like the book.

What I present in this chapter isn't just a list of derogatory opinions; it's an investigation into how they were formed. Because this kind of thinking doesn't happen overnight. It's like death by a thousand paper cuts, where the paper cuts are "stuff you hear and see on a daily basis" and death is "actively contributing to the stigma of mental illness." And that's as clean an analogy as you're going to get from me on this subject. Here we go.

Having a mental disorder is NOT normal.

As a baby, I suffered from seizures—not the shaking kind, but rather the horror-movie kind, where your eyes glaze over and your body freezes like someone's just pressed "pause" on you. I was rushed to the hospital, where the doctors ran a battery of tests and x-rays. It turns out I had something called petit mal, a type of epilepsy most commonly found in children, who eventually grow out of it. That's right, I grew out of seizures like they were night lights or dating people who treat you like shit (ok, so I only grew out of the seizures).

Fast-forward a few years to where I'm a teary-eyed seven-year-old sulking in my bedroom because some kid at school called me "mental." Upon hearing this, my dad says nothing and disappears for a few minutes. He returns triumphantly, holding a large yellow envelope. He looks weirdly excited as he reaches into the envelope and pulls out some dark-blue sheets of plastic. I'm confused and squint my eyes to pull focus. They're x-rays. "Look! We have proof that there's nothing wrong with your brain!" my dad squawks as he enthusiastically stabs at my mental blueprints. "And if anyone tells you any different, you can show them these and say, 'See! My brain is normal!'"

This was the first time I'd heard of a *normal* brain, meaning there was such a thing as an *abnormal* brain. And judging by my father's reaction, it was a good thing to have a normal brain; it was a good thing that I could prove to that kid, or anyone, that I was not mental. I had one of the good brains. Sure, my dad was trying to cheer me up, but let us for a moment imagine a seven-year-old Amanda walking into class clutching x-rays of her tiny skull and chanting, "I have a normal brain! I have a normal brain!" Because if that's not crazy, I don't know what is.

Growing up, I never encountered everyday, garden-variety mental illness. Whenever I heard or saw anything having to do with mental health, it was always an extreme (and often outdated) trope. For example, I saw my share of TV shows depicting grimy insane asylums filled with shadowy hallways that always had one flickering light for some reason. (Side note: Can we stop with the flickering asylum light? Just because we're crazy doesn't mean we're incapable of calling an electrician.) Whenever an example of mental illness came up, whether through TV, school, friends, parents, or strangers on the street, it was presented as something bizarre or out of the blue. Whatever it was, it was outside the realm of normal, and we all know there is nothing worse than anything outside the realm of normal.

Normality was a warm, cozy log cabin with a fireplace, hot chocolate, and Jonathan Taylor Thomas (I was young and had dreams). Abnormality was the raging blizzard outside that rained down icy daggers of shame. All I had to do was stay inside, and I'd be fine. It never occurred to me I wouldn't have a say in the matter. I assumed people got depression because they were just that "type" of person, and based on what I knew at the time, that type of person was a white woman aged twenty-five to fifty-five. It was about 79 percent white women and 21 percent white men. Luckily, I'm an Asian Jew, so there couldn't possibly be anything psychologically wrong with me! Hahaha, how I laugh at the mere insinuation! Little did I know none of that mattered, because guess who doesn't care what race, religion, or gender you are? *Britney voice*: It's mental illness, bitch.

Therapy is a waste of time. It's for people who love talking about themselves and for perverts.

From the ages of eight to thirteen, I attended a private boarding school in the UK, which was just like Hogwarts only without the magic. We saw our parents once every two weeks for a weekend. It was during one of those elusive visits when my parents told me they were getting a divorce. I cried for approximately eleven minutes, not out of sadness, more out of duty. I thought it was the right thing to do and eleven minutes was the right amount of time to spend doing it. By minute twelve, I was back to my usual self, only better. I was relieved, like super relieved, like been-holding-it-for-an-hour-and-finally-found-a-toilet relieved.

I was born in Hong Kong to a Chinese mother and a white, British father. My mother worked at a bank, and my father worked in advertising. They got married during their lunch breaks and went back to work right after, and they've been happily together ever since. Just kidding; they had a terrible marriage, which ended in divorce about eight years later. But the lunch break thing was true.

At the time I was the only kid at my school whose parents were divorced. It was the early nineties, so it wasn't Chill & Good yet. Nowadays, when someone tells me their parents are still together, I gasp in horror and ask if everything's ok. Back then, divorce was a rare jewel nobody talked about because it glimmered with depravity and shame, like a 42-carat diamond owned by Eva Braun.

Contrary to what you may think, my parent's divorce is *not* my mental illness origin story. Their divorce was the best thing to happen to our family. I'm grateful they split when they did because living in a house with parents who hate each other is not ideal. It's like living with two honey badgers, seemingly pleasant and cute until one of them breathes loudly, then everyone gets their face bitten. My parents weren't happy together, and I wanted them to be happy. Simple. However, my parents weren't big on "open and honest conversations." What they lacked in "talking about feelings" they more than made up for by engaging in canon divorce behaviors—passive aggression, angry stage whispering, and light psychological warfare. As delightful as that all was, I don't blame my parents for not wanting to discuss "family business." They grew up in families where talking about feelings wasn't common practice, where vulnerability was seen as weak and unbecoming, where children were seen and not heard (and also rarely seen), where televisions didn't exist, but when they did, they didn't have REMOTES. Upsetting times, we can all agree. The point is, these behaviors didn't spring from nowhere; they were passed down, like heirlooms. But instead of a handmade quilt, the legacy is generations of families not able to talk about feelings. Or it is a handmade quilt, and each square is a toxic phrase like "Stop Crying" and "You'll Be Fine" and "Nobody Likes a Sad Girl." Ok, I should make this quilt. It sounds awesome.

Anyway! My parents, yes. When it came to something as emotionally fraught as divorce, which was still a fledgling concept at the time, my parents were ill-equipped to help me navigate the fallout. They genuinely wanted to help, and it's not like they didn't *want* to talk to me, I think they just didn't know how. So they did the next best thing and paid a stranger to do it. I was bundled off to therapy—and this, this was the radioactive spider bite.

It doesn't escape me that I was incredibly fortunate my parents had the funds and wherewithal to send me to a child therapist. It was the best thing they could do for me—and I HATED IT.

When you're allowed to see your parents only once every two weeks, every hour counts. Now one of those hours was being used up in the presence of some stranger who was NOT my parent and was asking me about MY GODDAMN BUSINESS. At first, I told the truth, "I'm fine with the divorce!" (the children's version of "I'm not crazy!"). The therapist didn't buy it and assumed I was covering up my true feelings, because what kind of child is happy about their parents splitting up? A demonic monster child, that's what!

I spent hours sitting in that beige office, which could be described only as a really beige office. Classic therapist office art hung from the walls—the typical abstract, floral, or African (but painted by a white person) prints. In an attempt to make it "kid friendly," there was a small wooden table in the corner of the room accompanied by two little wooden chairs on either side. Perched atop the table was a small, colorful abacus. I remember looking at it and thinking, "If you're a kid who *chooses* to play with an abacus, then maybe you *should* be here." (Side note: I played with the abacus.) Tattered, old children's books were strewn on the floor around the table. To the untrained eye it looked messy, but to me, a genius, it looked like a deliberate delineation between child and adult territory.

I imagined other kids sitting at that table, flipping through *Tommy Goes to Church Again!* while having to describe an unrelenting inner pain using words they didn't even know existed. Children my age, traumatized by their parent's divorce, who had to sit in this beige box with this stranger and this abacus and crack open their fragile hearts while their parents pressed their ears against the door in the other room, desperate to hear which one of them was to blame for all this.

I'd been in therapy for a few weeks and was tired of being mentally poked and prodded. I was tired of being made to feel like a liar. So I started to lie. I lied about lying about being ok. I made up some crap about feeling torn and upset. I told the therapist what I thought they wanted to hear, and you know what? It worked. The therapist backed off, and I didn't feel ashamed anymore. A few crocodile tears here, a couple of "I'm sad today"s there, and I was out. The whole experience taught me three things:

1. Therapy is bullshit.
2. Never tell anyone your true feelings.
3. Abacuses can be fun.

I steered clear of therapists after that. But a couple of years later, when I was scouring my dad's bookcase, as I often did, I found a book written by someone called Sigmund Freud. I was drawn to it because it had a green cover and the guy on the front looked like Santa. The book was called *Case Histories 1: 'Dora' and 'Little Hans.'* I thought it must be some sort of delightful German fairy tale storybook! COOL!

Reader, it was not cool. For one, there was a lot more horse penis than I expected. I asked my father why on earth he owned this little book of horrors. He informed me that Freud was the most famous psychiatrist in the world and explained that this Freud character had developed the psychoanalytic theory of personality development, which argues that personality is formed through the conflicts of the id, the ego, and superego. Ok fine, but what does that have to do with equestrian peen? Was "horse-penis envy" part of *everyone's* persona? (Only later did I find out that, yes, it very much is.)

The more I learned about Freud, either from books or through hacky portrayals in TV and film, the more I believed he was some sort of dirty sex pervert and the people who went to therapy were dirty sex perverts and all they wanted to do was have dirty sex with their mothers.

I was eleven and never going back to therapy.

People with depression are lazy attention-seekers, who lie in bed all day and do NOTHING.

At nine years old, I asked a teacher what *depressed* meant.

"Where did you hear that word?" she asked.

I said, "I read it in a book."

She paused. "It's like sad."

I was a precocious little turd, so whenever I learned a big-sounding word I used it constantly. At school, anytime friends looked sad, I'd tell them they looked depressed. I was a great friend. I started to call everything sad-looking depressed. Pugs? Depressed. Crying babies? Depressed. Kevin Costner? Depressed. (*Waterworld* had just come out, so I may not have been too off base there.) One time I asked a teacher if he was ok because he looked depressed, and the look on his face—my god, it was like I'd straight up asked him if he enjoyed licking public handrails.

"You shouldn't use that word, Amanda."

"Why?"

"Because it doesn't mean what you think it means."

"What does it mean?"

"Something else."

Why could no one explain this word? I decided not to use it again till I could work out its true meaning. Based on my teacher's reaction, this depression thing was mortifying.

Over the next few years, through TV shows and friends' "wiser" older siblings, I learned that being depressed didn't mean sad. It meant VERY sad. So sad that you didn't want to get out of bed! (Not *couldn't* get out of bed—*didn't*. I still saw it as a choice.) I heard rumors of depressed people not leaving their bed for days on end. I couldn't understand it. First of all, being in bed is awesome; second of all, if you don't like it, get up; and third of all, if you stopped lounging about all day then maybe you wouldn't be depressed. Ever thought about that? You are welcome.

From the ages of nine to nineteen I assumed that depression was a bed-based illness of the apathetic. In my mind, depressed people were lazy, antisocial oafs whom you wouldn't want to be friends with because they were clearly no fun. There was no such thing as an entertaining, active depressed person. Depressed people didn't party; depressed people didn't even LAUGH. Why would I want to be friends with a surly hermit? (Side note: a thing I now am.)

At sixteen, I saw depression as nothing more than a sneaky tactic to garner sympathy from us good, mentally well folks. My initial curiosity for depression quickly curdled into anger and bitterness. It was like, "Listen, we'd all looove to spend the day in bed, but we can't, because we have shit to do, and nobody is going to pick up after you, so get up!" It pissed me off that these slackers thought they could get away with doing nothing just because they were sad.

Had I met a depressed person yet? Great question, and the answer was I didn't need to. I knew their game, with their unwashed hair and their no-can-do attitude. I see you, depression, I SEE YOU.

In retrospect, I had met hundreds of depressed folks and never knew it. I didn't know about high-functioning depression because (a) I never bothered to learn about it and (b) no one talked about it. I'd simply zeroed in on one small part of depression, making it about that single thing. I could've picked up a book and discovered its complexities and the different ways it manifests itself, but I didn't. Instead, I reduced depression to a one-dimensional character who didn't want to get out of bed.

I vowed to myself that if (god forbid) I ever contracted depression, I wouldn't spend my days in bed—HELL NO. I'd fight it off by getting out there! Go to parties, hang out with friends, maybe take up a hobby like pottery and clay the cray away. I wouldn't sit in a dark room feeling sorry for myself. I'd actually do something, like—uh, I dunno—CHOOSE TO BE HAPPY.

Mentally ill people are scary and wildly unpredictable, like ostriches or phone calls, and must be AVOIDED at all costs.

I can't even remember the first time I thought, "Mental people are scary." There wasn't a turning point or a come-to-Jesus moment—which would've been hard for me since I'm (a) Jewish and (b) not sexually attracted to Jesus. I just knew there was something spooky about them because people would always point them out as if they were feral, exotic creatures.

If you were in line at a grocery store and the person in front was shouting at a cashier, there was always some dude behind you who'd mumble, "Somebody's got some mental issues." If you saw a woman scream, cry, or express any emotion in public, there was always someone, most likely a male, who'd walk by and mouth the word "crazy," much to the amusement of gawking onlookers. Any bad driver outside the car you were in was a "goddamn lunatic." And it was scientific fact that every single homeless person was severely mentally disturbed. Growing up, I never questioned the validity (or lack thereof) of these statements. I was just relieved that crazy people could be easily identified, because if there's one thing scarier than a vocal mental person, it's a silent one. Luckily (to me), every symptom was loud and splashy. Even depression and anxiety had signage: depressed people looked like crestfallen zombies, and people with anxiety bit their nails, hyperventilated, and talked like they were cold. Easy.

By the time I entered my teens, I could spot and diagnose a mentally ill person a mile away.

It was like an episode of *Planet Earth*, but instead of animals it was people and instead of David Attenborough it was me . . . doing an impression of David Attenborough. "Here she is, the thirty-year-old female, having what appears to be a breakdown in the mall. Notice the shrillness of her voice, the wildness in her eyes, the tears streaming down her puffy cheeks. This is what is commonly known as *crazy*."

Little did I know that this behavior is *not* crazy and that women are allowed to have feelings whenever and wherever they damn well please. Little did I know that I should have asked her if she was ok because maybe she needed a sympathetic person rather than a judgy one. Little did I know this would soon be me.

I was in my early teens when I first heard the term *bipolar*. My mother told me about a friend of a friend who was bipolar. I remember thinking it sounded pretty cool, like a combination of *bionic* and *polar*. Like part robot, part bear.

To be fair, my mother did start the conversation by saying she didn't know "all the details," which is always a good sign that what you're about to hear is going to be a sizzling hot mess. She told me that this person's name was Jackie**, and that one time Jackie drove her car into a wall because she was bipolar. I was like what the fuck? (Not out loud. My mom isn't white.) It turns out, Jackie's bipolar convinced her that she was invincible, so to test that theory she drove her car into a wall. She survived, but apparently she often did stuff like that. I couldn't even fathom doing something like that *once*, let alone often!

In addition to Jackie's suicide missions, she also went on massive shopping sprees. Not fun sprees where you buy a minidisc player *and* a Motorola two-way pager (it was the year of our lord, Y2K); Jackie bought EVERYTHING she could get her hands on, including more cars, presumably to crash into more walls. Jackie couldn't afford any of this stuff. She maxed out her credit cards and went into debt, all because of this devilish bipolar curse! It was like listening to a scary story around a campfire.

"But how is she still alive?" I asked.

"Oh, she's not like that all the time," my mother replied flippantly. "Sometimes she's fine. These are just episodes that come up now and then."

Uh . . . EXCUSE YOU? There's a type of mental illness that can look TOTALLY NORMAL but then SOMETIMES makes you want to CRASH YOUR CAR INTO WALLS? It was so much misinformation to take in. Technically my mother had told me the truth, but there was no follow-up about how millions of people with bipolar lead "normal" lives with the help of medication and therapy. These were just cherry-picked sound bites, which in my mind boiled down to "Jackie: normal on the outside, madder than a box of frogs on the inside."

My god, this woman was a ticking time bomb. Jackie encapsulated all my worst fears about mentally ill people. I knew they were dangerous, but that wasn't the most horrifying thing; the most horrifying thing was that they could *look* normal.

They walked among us.

Medication is for PSYCHOPATHS and hilarious one-liners.

I'm sixteen, and my brother passes away. Everything happened fast—the death, the funeral, the speed at which people brought food to our house. I was given a "happy pill," a.k.a. Celexa, an antidepressant. It didn't make me feel any different, but I also didn't feel anything. I had completely shut down. Not in a robotic way— scarier than that. I had shut down to the point where you'd never know that my brother had just died. You'd think I was a content, polite, and rather sociable young lady.

I didn't see a therapist, because, as my childhood proved, they did not work. Instead, I went to people who were guaranteed to work—psychics. There was one psychic, Susan***, she looked like a sculptor from North Berkeley who owns chickens and grows sour apples in her backyard. Susan worked in a tiny room in the back of a spiritual gift shop. You had to dodge many a feathered dream catcher just to get to her office/closet.

Susan assured me that my brother was "doing well" in heaven, like she was a teacher at a PTA meeting for dead kids. I wanted to know if there was any way we could see him again. She told me if I wanted to see my brother all I had to do was repeat his name to myself before falling asleep, and he'd appear in my dreams. Seems legit, right? Wrong. Hate to break it to you, but it didn't work. And guess what? I didn't care. As long as Susan kept feeding me false-hoods in her confident, soothing tones, then I was all ears. Susan relayed a ton of "messages" from the "other side," and I lapped it all up because I was grieving, and lonely, and my heart wouldn't stop hurting. Although a small part of me knew Susan was fabricating a lot, nay, everything, it didn't matter because it did what child-hood therapy failed to do—made me feel better. Was it healthy? No. Would it have damaging long-term effects? Absolutely. But did it temporarily stop the inexhaustible bone crushing grief that I was both trying to repress and refrain from allowing it to consume my entire being? A little.

There was only one thing Susan said which disturbed me. She told me *my* first child would be my brother reincarnate. At any age that shit will mess you up, but at sixteen when your brother has *just* died and you're trying to stay sane, well that shit will fuck you all the way up till you're thirty. But people grieve in their own way. And, just like with mental illness, if you're not hurting others or yourself, then do whatever *you* need to do to feel better.

Eventually, I stopped visiting the psychics and taking the "happy pills," but the grief didn't stop. It divided and multiplied, and I didn't know what to do with it, so I buried it. I buried my grief, my anger, and my brother.

A couple of weeks later, I was back at school pretending like everything was fine. I was desperate not to be treated differently; I just wanted things to go back to how they were. I was a semi-popular teenager with a full-popular, older boyfriend whom I'd recently lost my virginity to because I craved love and acceptance from a very young age. Aaaaaanyway, the first time my boyfriend and I saw each other after my brother died, he could barely look me in the eye. He mumbled something about how the death of my brother was a little "too heavy" for him and maybe we should "cool it." Before my brother's death, I was this fun-loving, happy-go-lucky gal. Now I was this whole situation. An effort-draining time suck. I was a Sad Girl now, and I wasn't worth the hassle.

I was furious. Furious at my boyfriend for being a heartless scumbag WHOM I WAS GOING TO MARRY, furious at myself for appearing weak and damaged, and furious at my brother for dying. I shook the last thought from my mind and came up with a game plan. Fuck "fragile Amanda"—fragility was not hot. It was time to introduce a new and improved Amanda, with 50 percent more jokes, sexual prowess and zero emotional baggage. Before I was burying my feelings, but now I was paving over them and building a Universal Studios Amanda—fun on the outside, wildly disappointing on the inside.

I never told my friends about the Celexa. If people even got a whiff of the fact that I'd taken antidepressants, I knew I'd be finished. Who wants to be friends with a psycho pill popper? It would ruin my social life, which at sixteen *was* my life. To protect my image, I needed to erase any semblance of the old Amanda and lean all the way into the new one. I needed a full, poorly thought out rebrand. I needed to be Dominos. Old Amanda was "Domino's Pizza," but new Amanda was now "just Dominos" because I was much more than pizza! Not that much more, but more.

To this day, people are uncomfortable talking about antidepressants and antipsychotics. There's still a shame attached to mind medication that you don't find with other lifesaving or pain-relief drugs. There's no shame in ibuprofen, Percocet, or Vicodin. The pain they treat is obvious. *Something* causes it; it has a concrete reason for being. And when you see someone in pain, you feel for them, and not just in a compassionate way; you actually *feel* for them. When you see someone stub their toe, you feel a phantom twinge in your toe. You wince instinctively, and a sense of camaraderie rushes through your unstubbed body, moving you to say something unhelpful like, "Oooh, I felt that."

It's an easy formula everyone can understand: person in visible pain + pain-relief medication x finite period of time = all better. The pills make sense because they treat something tangible. But you can't see what antidepressants treat, and what's more, we don't know how long it takes for them to "fix" the problem. You can't pop a pill every four hours for two days and it's gone. You've gotta take them every day for as long as it takes, and, in some cases, as long as it takes can be forever. When it comes down to it, the pills themselves aren't scary; they're merely physical manifestations of people's deeper fear, which is that they don't understand depression at all.

I spent my teens overcompensating and projecting my fears about medication onto other people. Examples:

- If someone got angry or raised their voice, I'd tell them to "take a chill pill" or "pop a Valium." I didn't know what Valium was, but I knew it calmed you down. Yeah, I'd seen *Requiem for a Dream*.

- If someone was being silly or laughing hysterically, I'd quip from the side of my mouth, "Looks like somebody forgot to take their meds today" or conversely "Looks like the meds are wearing off!" And oh, how we'd laugh and laugh.
- If I was confused, disorganized, or lacked focus, I'd jokingly scream, "I feel like I'm taking crazy pills!"—a line stolen directly from the sleeper hit of 2001, *Zoolander*. I also used "Sorry, the pills haven't kicked in yet," because *Zoolander* quotes got tired real quick.
- Thanks to *Prozac Nation*, if anyone looked a little down, I'd suggest "a Prozac . . . or four! Amirite?" with all the charm of an angry white guy working through some stuff at an open mic.

It became a self-fulfilling prophecy. I convinced myself that medication was ineffective and that its only redeeming quality was I could use it to shame and ridicule people. Medication wasn't for me; it was for psychos in the movies.

If you're mental, you'll never be able to get a job— or worse . . . A BOYFRIEND.

I was nineteen when I felt my mind begin to rot. I was depressed and often found myself reaching incredible new lows. But every time I landed in a dark place, I'd remember the promise I'd made to myself years before: fight the depression. So that's what I did. I went clubbing, got drunk, slept with random dudes, and hung out with an awesome group of friends. I was a regular, run-of-the-mill student. Super ordinary. Nothing to see here.

I had full-blown high-functioning depression, and it was working for me. All I had to do was concoct a completely separate version of myself through which I could project counterfeit thoughts and feelings, such as humor, passion, and basic human empathy. This freed up space in my other, real self, which I used as a landfill where I dumped all my garbage feelings. I could dump and dash without any consequences, and it was awesome.

I had everyone fooled, including myself. Sure, it would've been better if I could've talked to people about how I was feeling, but that would have meant admitting I had depression, and I would rather die than do that—which was ironic, as I was beginning to experience suicidal ideation for the first time. I'd run out of space in my mind to store any more grief or trauma, and I'd run out of places to hide.

I'd been living in an absurd world of denial. I was like the Black Knight in *Monty Python and the Holy Grail*, and every time a chunk of my mind broke off I'd defiantly assert, "'Tis but a scratch!"

I needed to do something to stall this mind rot. I wasn't a teenager anymore; at twenty whole years old, I was a proper adult. I summoned up the courage to visit the university GP and gave him a condensed version of recent events. He wanted to refer me to a psychiatrist, because while he wasn't an "expert," he said it sounded like I was demonstrating signs of bipolar.

Smash cut to the recesses of Amanda's mind.

BIPOLAR . . . BIPOLAR BIPOLAR BIPOLAR BIPOLAR. Where have I heard that before? Think, Amanda, THINK! Oh god, that crazy woman Mum told me about, the one who crashed cars and bought things. OH SH—

Smash cut back to doctor's office.

I nodded as he handed me a number to call, or maybe he scheduled an appointment for me? I'm not sure. I was in a haze of confusion and terror. Was I not . . . normal? I rang my mother straightaway and told her everything. She was silent, and I could tell it wasn't supportive silence because supportive silence on a phone is not a thing. Before I could ask if she was still on the line, she proceeded to scold me for going to the doctor in the first place.

She was furious. She told me that this doctor's appointment was now on my "record," and it was likely that bipolar was now on my "record," and future employers wouldn't hire me because of the bipolar on my "record." To answer your question, no, I did not know what record she was talking about, and I still don't. But I did know one thing—I'd messed up my entire life with a single doctor's visit. My mother confirmed all my greatest fears about mental illness: it was shameful, it could ruin your life, and IT WAS NOT NORMAL. In Asian culture, having a "proper" job (a lucrative 7:00 a.m.–8:00 p.m. conducted in a professional office setting) is essential, more so than food or water. Your job is your identity, and without a respectable job identity then what are you? A writer? HAHAHA! Honestly, can you imagine?

My mind began to whir. If I couldn't get a job with bipolar, then I definitely wouldn't be able to get ANYONE TO LOVE ME. Who would want to marry an unemployed insane person? No one! My only two goals in life (getting a job and a human to commit to me forever) vanished, just like that. I started to tear up.

My mother's voice switched from disappointed to heist movie. "Here's what you're going to do," she said. "You're *not* going to go to that psychiatrist appointment, and you're never going back to that doctor. Got it?"

"Yes."

"Good. Everything else ok?"

The next time I talked about my mental health, I was in a psych ward.

Once a mental, ALWAYS a mental.

One of the main reasons I staved off the onslaught of mental illness for so long was because I knew if it "got" me, I'd have it forever. And I'm not talking about the fair-weather illnesses like depression or anxiety (which I still believed could be cured if you were willing to put the effort in). I'm talking about "proper" mental problems, the ones with serious medical names like schizophrenia, psychosis, and bipolar. The day a doctor diagnoses you with one of those bad boys, that's it—you're in for LIFE. And it's not a chill disease that pops up now and then like eczema or herpes. It's *always* there, and you just have to live with it, like a conjoined twin who constantly wants to kill you.

Why was I so terrified by these scary-name illnesses? At the time, I believed that your illness defined you. You could be anyone you wanted unless you had something like schizophrenia. Suddenly you're no longer Tisha, an entrepreneur who collects rare books; you're Tisha, the schizophrenic. That's your whole deal now. That's what people would think about when they thought about you.

I didn't want to *be* anything other than myself (and Beyoncé). And if I couldn't be myself (or Beyoncé), then I didn't want to be anyone.

Reaching Out
For Help, a.k.a.
A Fucking Nightmare

If you're someone who suffers from anxiety or is human, asking for help of any kind is painful.

Something as simple as asking for directions takes a certain amount of determination and careful planning. We've all been there—alone, on the street, holding a dead phone. You have no choice but to query a stranger to steer you in the right direction. But inquiring is the least of your worries because first you must pick the perfect stranger at the perfect time. You want someone who's local, about your age, and not a serial killer. Perfect. You lurch forward, stopping them in their tracks. They look at you like you're waving a giant dildo in their face. You panic but somehow manage to muster up the courage to bark, "Which way to the dildo repair shop?"

They hurry away, leaving you a little hurt and wondering what went wrong. Perhaps you need to reevaluate the approach? Maybe don't open with the dildo. Set some context. Ease people into it (I absolutely saw what I did there). But the rejection stings, and you vow never to ask for directions again. You'll fix your own damn dildo . . . for now.

Like many people, I grew up believing that asking for help was a sign of weakness. It showed that you couldn't do something yourself. Asking for someone's help was akin to saying, "Look at me, I'm a fragile idiot baby who is bad at doing things." At school I was horrible at math—still am. Thank god it's useless now. (I'm joking. Please don't write me hate mail in code; I won't be able to work it out.) But back then math was a big deal. I had friends who were good at math. I could have asked them to help me, but I didn't. I was scared and embarrassed, but why? These were my friends, not some stranger on the street, and that's what made it worse! At least I'd never have to see the stranger again. Would the memory of the encounter haunt me every day for the rest of my life? Of course! But at least it wouldn't be in my face the whole time. At least the stranger didn't know my family or friends or the guy I was secretly in love with, so there was no way it would get back to him that I was *audible gasp* bad at math.

Although asking for help in general can be excruciating, it's a fantasy getaway compared to reaching out to someone about your mental health. When it comes to day-to-day reaching out, once you have the answer it's over. Even if the answer is "I don't know," that conversation is DONE. When you ask someone at work how to use the printer, it doesn't mean there's something inherently wrong with you; it just means you're lazy because the instructions were in the email that was sent this morning, GARY. The point is, it's not personal. But when it comes to mental illness, everything is personal, and no conversation is ever DONE.

For most of my life, I've been ashamed of my mind and have gone to great lengths to hide my illness from everyone, including myself. I spent my formative years staunchly "powering through," which ultimately led to my first breakdown.

In college I focused all my mental strength on doing the least in terms of studying and doing the most in terms of having uninspired sex with mediocre men. I wanted to flood my mind with bullshit. I couldn't afford a lapse in distraction; my depression was too quick. It's like a toddler in Target. One minute they're calm and under control, the next they've run off into the mall. You don't know how long it will take to find them, or sometimes you're like "ah, fuck it" and just wait it out in the food court. You have no control over the situation. My depression will ghost me for days, even weeks. When I eventually do get hold of it, I'm relieved—not happy relieved, just relieved that I know where it is and can keep an eye on it. Just like a lost child.

Reaching out to my family was out of the question. I had stopped talking to my father when I was eighteen, and my mother had made her feelings clear on my situation. We rarely talked about our feelings, and I was fine with that.

I was lucky enough to have a bunch of great friends whom I could confide in. I'd been in boarding school since I was eight years old, so I like to think I was raised by friends rather than parents. I had plenty of opportunities to talk to friends about my burgeoning depression. It should have been easy given that I'd previously shared far more embarrassing personal shit. I'd shared diary entries, angsty teenage poetry, masturbatory habits, weird kinks (both sexual and nonsexual), petty grudges, the fact that I once had hemorrhoids— the list goes on. I love to overshare with close friends, and yet when it came to talking about something as straightforward as feeling sad, I couldn't do it. My friends knew me as "somewhat fun" and "up for a laugh." I didn't want to break the illusion; I didn't want our relationship to change. I was afraid that if one day I said, "I'm still fun, but sometimes I feel like killing myself," they'd treat me differ- ently because "Amanda's kinda…" then they'd widen their eyes like, "don't even go there." Sure, they'd still be my friends, but something would change. Parts of our friendship would be cordoned off like a crime scene or VIP area or VIP crime area. My overshare security clearance would be revoked. From that point on I'd be privy to only surface-level conversations. Over time, I'd drift apart from the group, and when asked about me they'd say, "Oh Amanda? Yeah, she's nice but she's a little . . ." and they'd make that face people do when they're like "sorry, can't help you there."

Did any of this happen? Of course not. But what wonderfully elaborate narcissistic fantasies I do weave! All this time I thought the problem was other people, which most of the time it is, but in this case, I had to take some responsibility. I had grossly overinflated the difficulty of reaching out. I had built it up as this monstrous undertaking, something that had several moving parts and required meticulous planning, like a mission to Mars or brunch. I thought disclosing one's unfit mental state involved drama and high production levels. There'd be pensive looks and soft lighting. It'd be similar to *The Bachelor*, but instead of declaring my unshakable yet super shakable love I'd be declaring a darkness that envelops my soul. As I said, similar.

It wasn't until I'd come to terms with my mental illness that I understood what reaching out for help meant. I realized it didn't have to be the full song and dance I'd composed and choreographed in my mind. I didn't have to open with the dildo and tell people I was depressed right out of the gate. I could try something simple like "Do you have a sec to chat? Not feeling great today." I forgot that it's just as important to ease yourself into these conversations as it is to ease others. I'd spent so much time worrying about how other people would react that it left no time for me to think about how I felt.

Still, just because reaching out doesn't have to be a whole thing doesn't mean it's not tough. Saying "I need help" is not easy. It has an unnatural mouthfeel, much like the word *mouthfeel*. Some people feel relieved after they've asked for help, like a burden has been lifted. I felt the opposite.

The actual asking never bothered me. I was more concerned with the subsequent fallout. The moment after the words tumble off your tongue. A second suspended in time while you frantically search for a reaction in the other person's eyes. Fuck. Was this a bad idea? You're hit with the urge to scoop the words off your chest like cookie crumbs and cram them back in your mouth, but all you can do is wait.

I'm lucky in that I've experienced only a handful of bad reactions to my requests for help. One that sticks out is the time I called my mother from a psychiatric hospital where I was an inpatient. It was November, and I was planning to fly home for the holidays. The plan was to stay with her and have a family Christmas. I'd been in and out of therapy and hospitals for a couple of months since my first suicide attempt, and this would be the first time I'd get to speak to my mother.

It didn't concern me that she hadn't been in touch; I assumed she was too distraught or busy, most likely the latter. I was excited to hear her voice and discuss plans for Christmas, but when the call connected my stomach dropped. Her tone was cold as she spat her words down the receiver. It took me a second to figure out what she was saying, because all I could think about was "Why is she mad at me? What did I do wrong?" The next thing I heard was something about the heating in her house being broken. There was no heat, and because I was "so fussy" about being warm I shouldn't stay with her. This was even more confusing. Sure, I'm always cold. I'm a woman; it's one of our greatest hits. But that wouldn't deter me from staying with my family. Also, it was November. Surely the heating would be fixed before I arrived. Also, WHAT? Why are we talking about the BLOODY HEATING? I was so confused, but it was what my mother said next that cleared everything up. She talked about my suicide attempt and how she didn't want *that kind of thing* in her house, and if I wanted to *try that kind of thing again,* then I should *stay in a hotel.* Now I understood. The call ended, and I wouldn't reach out again for years.

You'd think that encounter would have deterred me from reaching out to anyone ever again, but after I put down the phone I picked it back up and called my friend Tara. I'd known Tara and her family since we were eight years old. I hadn't spoken to her in a while. She answered the phone, and I said, "I'm coming home for Christmas. I'm not well, and I have nowhere to stay." She didn't need to hear any more. I stayed with Tara and her family, and it was one of the best Christmases I've ever had. I count myself lucky to have Tara and her family. It wasn't the first time they saved me and it wouldn't be the last.

That conversation with my mother spurred me to talk about my mental illness. It was strangely motivating, as though nothing could be worse than being shot down by your own mother. It's been years since that exchange took place, and it's taken me a while to process. To be completely honest, I made peace with it only in the last few weeks. Learning your child tried to take their own life must be one of the most heartbreaking and horrifying things a parent can hear. Couple that with an inability to articulate trauma thanks to the inherited heirloom quilt of repression, and it's no wonder my mother reacted the way she did. For years I thought she was angry at me—and she absolutely was—but when I look at it now, from way back here, I see she was grieving. Neither of us knew how to articulate our feelings, and it ripped us apart.

In the years that followed, the worst reactions I've had from people have been silent discomfort, and I get it. There's no guidebook on what to do when someone comes to you with a mental health issue. The best things you can do are be there, don't judge, and listen. Let them talk. Don't ask a bunch of questions or offer opinions, just shhhhhhh. And when your friend or loved one says they think they might have [insert mental illness], BELIEVE THEM. Don't dismiss it like, "Yeah, but everyone feels like that sometimes." Maybe they do, maybe they don't—who cares? The point is, someone has confided in you about their mental health. Do you know what that's like? It's a FUCKING NIGHTMARE, so take what they say seriously. Once they've finished talking, ask if there's anything you can do to help, and remind them you'll always be there if they want to chat. Now that you're aware of your friend's feelings, you'll know to check in on them more often because, and I can't stress this enough, it is *not* the responsibility of the person going *through it* to reach out to you. If you sense something may be up, go ahead and give them a call. Or better yet, text them; calls are horrifying. And don't feel like you have to be all "Hey, wanna talk about how you're all depressed and shit?" Simply talk to your friend how you would normally and try not to apply pressure for a response. If they want to reply, they'll reply.

For anyone reading this who's been too scared or embarrassed to talk to friends about your mental health, I know. I see you. This is a fucking nightmare. But the fact that you're even *thinking* about talking to someone means you're already halfway there. Reach out in your own way, whether it's in person or by phone, email, text, or DM, but do it soon. And if you're thinking about reaching out to a friend you're worried about, do it now. There's never a "wrong" time to reach out, any time is the right time. So, go on, drop them a text now. I'm here. I'll wait.

Trying to Make
the Shit Stop

(Trigger warning: this chapter is about suicide.)

There's a line in the movie *Girl, Interrupted* where the protagonist, Susanna Kaysen, talks about her suicide attempt. She explains that she didn't try to kill herself; she was "trying to make the shit stop." And honestly, that's the closest I've come to explaining myself.

I've been open about my mental health for years, but the one topic I seem to avoid is suicide. It's not that I don't want to talk about it. I do. It's important. I've just never figured out *how*. The issue of suicide is so personal and fraught with anguish that it's hard to make any part of it, for want of a better word, relatable.

I understand that not everyone reading this will have been personally affected by suicide, but most people know how it feels when a celebrity takes their own life. Whether you care about them or not, people are for the most part shocked and saddened. Even if you "saw it coming" (top tip: don't say this when someone has just died), it doesn't make it any less devastating. Even before details are released, people love to speculate as to why. Why did they choose to kill themselves? Why, when they had so much to live for? Why would they do this to their friends and family?

There are so many misconceptions around suicide, mostly drummed up by those who've never encountered it. People are quick to question motives without taking the time to understand them. There's no short answer to "Why?" But that's what people want. Some don't have time to learn about the intricacies of other people's psyches and how these complexities brought them to the lowest point in their lives. Others just don't want to hear it. Suicide is at once so unfathomable yet so painfully real. People need to keep it at arm's length just to wrap their heads around it. They want to hear one or maybe two simple explanations, like "addiction" or "drinking and depression" or "stress." The end of a life reduced to an easy(ish)-to-digest sound bite. And who better to feed us than the media.

The media aren't as interested in the *whys* as much as they are the *hows*. They tend to focus more on the ghoulish details rather than discussing the struggles that can lead to such tragic ends. Of course they do! It's what boosts ratings. Feeding the public's morbid fascination is nothing new; remember, "If it bleeds it leads!" That said, there are guidelines in place for how to report on suicide that many news outlets now follow. We can't blame the media for everything, because when it comes down to it, suicide is scary. Even seeing the word written down makes me feel a little uneasy. By no means do I intend to try to make the topic of suicide "fun" when I write about it. I just want to make it easier for us to talk about. And for that to happen, we (not just the media) need to work on a few things:

- We need to be proactive in educating ourselves on mental health and suicide. Most of us have access to the internet and libraries, so this shouldn't be a stretch.
- We need for those who've either survived or been affected by a suicide to share their experiences (if they can).
- Upon hearing that someone has taken his or her own life, we must try to be a little slower to judge.

I can't speak for celebrities or anyone else. But I can clear up some common misconceptions about suicide based on my experience.

When people hear of someone's death by suicide, they immediately wonder why the person "chose" to die. This has always struck me as strange—the idea that suicide is a choice. Like we have a Cheesecake Factory menu's worth of options but decide, "Screw it! It's my cheat day. I'll have the tragic death by my own hand." Often, people don't feel like they have a choice. That's how most of us end up in the position of contemplating or attempting suicide. If we felt like there was even the slightest chance we could avoid being in that situation, we would take it. Suicide was never my first "choice." Dying was never my goal. I was simply trying to find a way out of my mind.

My first suicide attempt came as a shock to everyone, including me. In the days leading up to it, I felt fine. I was twenty-seven and working in San Francisco. I had the privilege of a well-paying job which allowed me to exist in the Bay Area, and that's exactly what I did. I hardly went out. I had a handful of friends all of whom were from work. All I did was shuttle to and from work only stopping to eat and smoke. But that "existence" had nothing to do with me being a Sad Bitch and everything to do with being a little shit. My mental illness is not to blame for me not joining comedy sketch groups, writing for live theater shows, and making life-long friends in SF's creative community, because I did all of those things a couple of years later while still VERY MENTAL. But for now, my illness lay dormant.

My best friends, Beth and Raza, had come to San Francisco to visit me from the UK, and I was excited to see them. I looked and acted SUPER normal, which was probably a good sign that I was NOT NORMAL AT ALL.

I'd spent most of my life trying to outrun mental illness, but unbeknownst to me those running days were over. My mind brimmed with trauma and depression, like a pressure cooker I'd unknowingly left turned on for a decade. But instead of everything spilling over, it exploded.

At the time, I was in an intense and wildly toxic relationship. My self-esteem was at all-time low, and my ability to distinguish between love and hate had all but disappeared. Love *was* hate, and hate was more hate. Like a ravenous dog, I feasted on occasional scraps of affection that were tossed at me between long periods of gaslighting. I had no idea whether I was coming, going, or standing still. I can look back now with some clarity about the turmoil I was in, but at the time I was like THIS IS GREAT. I blew past every red flag like a slalom skier with a death wish. I was determined to make it work with this person even though his ambivalence toward me had reached comical levels of apathy. He didn't want me, but he didn't want to let me go. A rational person would see this and say, "I'm out." I saw it and said, "It's love."

We fought a lot. The night of my suicide attempt we fought. There was nothing new or unusual about this particular argument, but something about it cracked me open from the inside. This wasn't about the fight or the relationship. My mind had decided enough was enough. It was so full of trauma and depression from the past ten years that there wasn't any space left to fit a trivial spat. I can't recall what was said; all I can remember is the feeling. My eyes went dark, and my ears filled with the sound of a thousand static televisions. The only thing I could see was a movie reel, not unlike in *A Clockwork Orange*, but instead of world atrocities it showed repressed memories from my life. Memories I'd buried out in the back and grown trees over. Memories that, to this day, I can't bring myself to unpack. All of them relentlessly streamed into my consciousness. And just like Alex in *Clockwork*, I couldn't look away.

I was forced to not only watch but relive every harmful thought I'd ever had. Years' worth of trauma packed into a matter of minutes—or hours. I wasn't sure how long it lasted. I'd lost all concept of time. All I wanted to do was make the shit stop, and the only way I could was by shutting the whole thing down. Nothing else would work. In my mind, it wasn't a choice; it was the only option.

Eventually the volume on the TVs went down, and I was taken to the hospital. Looking back on it now, of course it wasn't the only option. But even with the benefit of hindsight, I will never say I had a choice. Feeling as though the only way to make the shit stop is to take one's own life is the loneliest feeling in the world. Perhaps things would have been different if I'd reached out to someone or if someone had told me, "I know." Because you can't ever know how it feels unless you've come out the other side. I feel fucking lucky to be alive. And if you're reading this and feel like you have no choice, I want you to know that I know. I see you. I love you, and I know. I'm not going to lecture you or give you advice—because honestly, that's the worst—but I am going to tell you that you're not alone. In fact, I'm going to tell you that a lot over the course of this book, so much so that you'll probably get sick of it.

Another phrase we hear a lot in regard to the news of a suicide is the person had "so much to live for"—Ok, what's your point? Are you saying they should have stayed alive because of all the stuff they could have done or experienced? It amazes me how some people are so quick to make blanket statements about the suicides of people they don't know. I understand you're trying to share your condolences, but words matter, and when you say, "it's a shame because they had so much to live for", you're shaming the victim for dying. You're saying it's sad they died because look at all the achievements and the stuff and the things, they should have stuck around for all the things!

At the time of my writing this chapter, news just broke of Kate Spade's suicide, and already there are a flurry of tweets, "But her patterns were so colorful and fun!" and "But she was so successful!" These people can't fathom why someone who seemingly "had it all" could ever "throw it all away." There MUST be an explanation, and we MUST have it! But before you ask to speak to the manager about a celeb's suicide, know this—there absolutely is an explanation and you're absolutely not entitled to it.

Also what does that mean for those who aren't successful, wealthy, household names? Is suicide understandable then? Mental illness doesn't discriminate; it doesn't give a shit who you are or how much money you have.

When it comes to mental health, we have no idea what people are going through, so we should never assume. People are shocked by suicide because they think it could never happen to them or anyone they know—as though it happens only to famous people or addicts. But when it does happen to someone they know, those same people might say the person "seemed fine" or "there weren't any signs." What signs? I smiled and laughed on the day of my suicide attempt. There aren't always signs. The best thing you can do is check in on your friends, even if you don't suspect anything, but especially if you do.

My second suicide attempt was less explosive and sudden than the first, but the two shared similar characteristics. It happened around a year later, in the summer. I'd managed to cobble my life together. It wasn't perfect, but it was good enough. I was in therapy and getting used to a slew of different meds. I was also in a newish relationship with my now husband. Although I'd spent the year unpacking the previous year, I hadn't even scraped the surface of my depression. The seemingly insurmountable nature of taking it on made me only more depressed. I would routinely take stock of my life to gain some perspective. I had my own apartment, was in therapy, was on medication, and had a boyfriend. Three of those things were luxuries I was privileged to have. So why wasn't any of it working? I'd think, "There are people who have it so much worse. I shouldn't be complaining. Maybe I'm not depressed. Maybe I'm just a whiny li'l bitch." I questioned why I was in therapy, and I questioned my meds, which didn't seem to be working. In fact, all they did was make me feel sleepy and gain ten pounds.

I wanted immediate results. I needed the therapy and medication to fix me up and spit me out as quickly as possible. I didn't put the work in. I just showed up, swallowed, and expected progress (yes, I did just make a sex joke in a chapter about suicide, and no, I am not better than that). I wasn't interested in getting well. I was focused on getting "back to normal." In a matter of months my depression folded in on itself, creating a supermassive black hole. Instead of matter, feelings would be sucked in and destroyed, making me impervious to the entire spectrum of human emotion. But because I'd formed a shiny outer shell, no one was any the wiser. Some people describe the descent into darkness as "spiraling," but I'd describe mine as more "floating away into nothingness." There was nothing aggressive or angry about my suicidal ideation; it was completely hopeless. I didn't even feel darkness, just an all-consuming void. I felt composed of skin and nothing else—no bones, no flesh, no blood, no life. As I lay in my bed on a mild day in June, I calmly decided there was only one option.

That was in 2014, and I haven't attempted suicide since. Have I had suicidal thoughts? Absolutely. But I haven't acted on them, thanks to a combination of medication, working hard in therapy, and reaching out to others for help. Fighting against a mind that is actively trying to kill you is exhausting. It takes work, but it's not impossible. There's no single big fix, but there are small things I do that help alleviate the strain. Everyone is different and what works for me may not work for you, but whatever it is, as long as you're not hurting yourself or others, do it.

Whenever I feel the steam rising in my head, I'll call a friend. I don't talk about suicidal ideation though; I just gossip and chat shit. It reminds me that I'm a person—a petty, *alive* person. And there's someone on the other end of this phone who cares enough to indulge me and my nonsense.

There's also the option to talk to a complete stranger at the National Suicide Prevention Lifeline by calling 1-800-273-8255 or if you're a young LGBTQ+ person there's The Trevor Project 1-866-488-7386 . Helplines work for some people. Find what works for you. But know this—you are not alone.

You are not alone.

You are skin, and flesh, and bone, and blood, and you are loved. And you are not alone.

This isn't about trying to make the shit stop. The shit will always be there. It's about managing it so that it never starts, comes back, or takes you down.

A quick guide on how to talk about suicide

- Do not use the word "committed"; instead, use "died by suicide" or "took his/her own life."
- Do not refer to a suicide attempt as "successful," "unsuccessful," or as a "failed attempt."
- Do not include or describe methods used.
- Do not speculate as to why the person took his or her own life. Don't be all "But she was so successful!" or "But he was always so happy!"

- Don't ask how this could have happened, because there isn't one straightforward answer. As the CDC puts it, "Suicide is never the result of a single factor or event, but rather results from a complex interaction of many factors and usually involves a history of psychosocial problems."
- Always include information about the National Suicide Prevention Lifeline 1-800-273-8255 and the Crisis Text Line 741-741.

If you are a journalist, you can find more resources on how to report on suicide on the following websites.

- **Reporting on Suicide:** reportingonsuicide.org
- **American Foundation for Suicide Prevention:** afsp.org
- **Centers for Disease Control and Prevention:** cdc.gov

PART 2

AD (After Diagnosis)

Safety in Numbness

You know when the dentist numbs your mouth with lidocaine for a tooth-procedure thing (I haven't been to the dentist in years) and for the next few hours you can't feel your tongue? I love that feeling—feeling like you can't feel. Your tongue lolling around your lips like a hot dog in the wind. You try to bite down, and instead of hurting, it's a cushioning sensation, like you're sinking your teeth into a wet, dense cloud. You try to chew the sides of your mouth, and it's the same. You know the pain is in there somewhere, lurking beneath the anesthesia, but for this brief shining moment, you can rest easy. There's no suffering here, only hot dogs and clouds and sweet, sweet lidocaine, ahhhhh.

Now imagine all that, but your tongue is your brain.

Being numb doesn't get a lot of play in depression culture. When people think of depression, they think of the major players, such as sadness, crying, tiredness, and just generally looking miserable—all things that involve feeling or expression. And while all forms of depression are valid, my favorite has to be numbness. It's like being wrapped in a blanket made from cashmere and denial, the comfiest combination in the known universe. Numbness, by its very nature, is not a feeling; it's a place. An escape where there's nothing to do but bathe in a false reality, like Palm Springs.

Numbness can manifest itself in different ways. There's the standard "no feeling." There's also "not feeling the appropriate feelings" and its sister strain "having feelings but not processing them in the correct way." No matter which one engulfs you, the effect is the same: dissociation.

Like many teenagers, I went through a phase of thinking "being into shit" was deeply uncool. When I was thirteen, I was cast in a main role for our school's production of the very old and very white musical *Half a Sixpence*. It was cool to be part of the school play, but it wasn't cool to *act* in it. I was dating a boy at the time; when I say dating, I mean sometimes we held hands. His name was David (it wasn't), but he went by "Dave" because of course he did (he didn't). He was white, tallish, and had a mop of mousy brown hair parted expertly into curtains. The most important thing was that he was popular. Had he dated every single girl in my year before he agreed to date me? Yes. But did he like me more than all the other girls in my year? Absolutely not. It's fair to say, I was way more into Dave than he was into me—a pattern that would continue well into my twenties.

Dave had a minor role in the play. I believe he had only a couple of lines, which he delivered poorly. One day, we had a rehearsal that required the entire cast to be there. During rehearsals, if you weren't in a scene, you sat in the audience. Dave and his friends had not seen me 'act' before. In one scene, the main male character has to break up with me because he's in love with another woman and I had to cry. Uh, consider it DONE. Even at the tender age of thirteen, I could Daniel Day-Lewis the shit out of crying about being dumped by a boy. But when the moment came for me to showcase my acting chops, I froze. I remembered that Dave was in the audience, so instead of letting loose I held back. I decided to be a chill and act like I wasn't acting.

The drama teacher, whom I loved and admired, stopped the scene and challenged me as to why I wasn't "doing it like we'd rehearsed before." I could see she was hurt, but all I did was shrug and mutter something puerile like, "Keep your knickers on."

This was the first time I realized I could shut down. The fallout of my parent's divorce had proved that I could switch emotions, but now I could turn them off like a tap. Again, a lot of teenagers go through this too-cool-for-school phase. At that age, indifference is king, especially when it comes to impressing friends and crushes. I hope this isn't the case now, but I don't know any teenagers, and even if I did, I'd be too afraid to ask them. Eventually, people grow out of it and spend the rest of their lives discovering and rediscovering what it's like to care about shit. I did not grow out of it. Well, I did and I didn't. I did spend the rest of my formative years twisting myself into a pretzel for guys who weren't into me. I did suffer from abandonment issues that made having any relationship, friend or partner, pretty precarious.

I prioritized "fitting in" over other menial things like "working hard" and "feeling good." And the way I did that was by shutting down. I'd grown out of trying to impress others with my no-can-do attitude, but I held onto its core functionality. In the past I'd dissociated to show I didn't care; now I did it for self-preservation. The process was the same.

My head, once filled with melodrama, fun, and weird sex stuff, was being infiltrated by a toxic sludge. Up until then, I'd become pretty good at repressing trauma, but by the time I got to college my skills had started to wane. The cracks in my mind deepened, and the sludge began to seep out. The repression wasn't working! I needed something stronger. Denial was a feeble gateway drug. I needed hard-core anesthesia, and that's exactly what I got.

For nearly a year I lived in the Palm Springs of my mind, and it was wonderful. I was tan and warm on the outside and completely cold and bare on the inside. Nothing could touch me, because I was nothing. I stopped going out to all the parties and clubs and the bottle service with the—ok, I can't do this. You know I never went out before. I just thought I needed to "sex up" this chapter a little bit. Oh well.

I continued to stay in but stopped maintaining friendships, which was huge, since for most of my life my friends were my family. I'd also rekindled a highly toxic relationship with my high school boyfriend, which was fun, as his clear hatred for me never registered. One time he played me a song that he said reminded him of us and I shit you not the song was literally about how this guy wanted to get rid of his girlfriend but didn't know how. And when the song was over, I was like "omg that's so sweet I love how songs remind you of us." Yep. Wow. You know that horrendous saying "It is what it is"? I was the physical embodiment of that phrase—just pure, beige nonsense.

Little did I know that while my body floated on a sea of quiet dissociation, my mind was wreaking havoc on itself. At least with repression I was able to feel guilt and shame. Every time I buried a dark thought, I'd feel a twinge of grief, like I was having a little funeral for each one. The mourning period was swift, around two seconds, but at least I felt something. By contrast, this numbing agent blacked me out. For all I knew, this was my life now—oblivious, carefree, and existing purely as an idea for men who've never been to therapy, like a manic pixie dream girl, only without the dream or the pixie. That's the thing with numbness: you think it's saving you, when really it's saying to you, "Look over there, it's Beyoncé!" While burning your entire house to the ground with your back turned.

It takes a lot to leave Palm Springs, and it's often not your choice. For me, it felt like a kidnapping. The only thing that could cut through my numbness was white-hot depression. A depression so potent it could singe your nose hair from a mile away.

From nine years old, my depression had morphed and fluctu-
ated. Now, at age eighteen, it was taking on a new form. This new
depression mushroomed after months of being locked up. I'd left it
untended and given it room to grow wild, like a garden, more Grey
than Secret. It seared right through me. Even though the mental
anguish was unbearable, I felt grateful. It's a strange feeling because
you want to die, but for the first time in a while you feel alive. For
me, feeling something, even if it's utter shit, is better than feeling
nothing at all.

I've since continued to drift in and out of dissociation. Just
because you emerge from it once doesn't mean it won't pull you
back in. Mental illness isn't some monthly subscription box service
that turns up in neatly packed stages. It's more like an electrical
appliance with a delivery window of 8:00am – End of Time pm

All parts of mental illness are exhausting and agonizing, but in
my experience there's nothing more dangerous than numbness. It
boils you like a frog while simultaneously keeping you on ice.

I wish there were things I could suggest that would help, but
I've never found a way around it.

There's a fine line between being apathetic and being unwell.
So if you ever find yourself isolated from the rest of the world but
you're fine with it, you may not be fine at all. You may be in Palm
Springs.

For the record, I like Palm Springs. I've been there a couple of
times, and it's always been quite pleasant and deserty.

Quietly
Freaking Out

Anxiety is one of those "join the club" terms people like to throw around. *Depression* is easy to bandy about too, but anxiety is more universal, because isn't it just, like, being worried? Or nervous? Everyone has been worried or nervous at some point in their lives. We're born worried! Have you ever seen a newborn baby? They always look like they're in distress (understandable, as they've just been pulled out of a human body). From birth to death, we'll never stop having things to worry about. We're spoiled for choice. There are big things like climate change, poverty, racism, homophobia, transphobia, sexism, war. Then there are small things like making new friends, wondering if you've packed enough for a trip, or thinking about whether your therapist actually likes you or is just putting up with you, y'know, for the money. All super normal things to worry about. And that's why it's so easy to dismiss anxiety—because it's *so* normal.

But surely that's a good thing? Don't we want to normalize mental illness? Isn't that the goal of this whole book? Yes, yes, and no; the goal of this book is to make me rich and famous.

What's happened with anxiety is that its normalization has undermined the severity of its condition. There's a difference between feeling anxious and having anxiety. Over the years, the meanings and subtleties of what it means to have anxiety have been lost, swept away in a semantic whirlwind of *stress* and *panic*.

I'm anxious about a lot of things. From the moment I wake up till the moment I go to sleep, which is a couple of hours before I wake up again, I'm anxious. During the night, I worry about what will happen the next day, and then during the next day, I worry about what will happen later in the day, and so on and so forth. I'm convinced most people feel this way—maybe not all the time, but it makes me feel better to imagine they do. This is not a unique feeling, and it's one that can run in the background while you tend to other things. We spend our days worrying, but it doesn't stop us from doing things at work or around the house. And that's the difference. Anxiousness lets you get on with shit; anxiety doesn't let you do shit. Anxiousness has a raison d'être. Anxiety doesn't need a reason—it doesn't need anything. In the alignment system, anxiety is chaotic evil. It can bubble up from a specific spot in your soul, or it can come from nowhere. Sometimes you can feel it coming; other times it surprise tackles you to the ground from a nearby bush.

Having an anxiety disorder is like living in a haunted house. There are times when you're sitting in your living room, reading a book, and thinking, "This is cool. I like the quiet," and other times when you're washing dishes in the kitchen and you hear the front door slam and think, "Goddammit, I knew I'd die alone in this house." It's an exhausting way to live. Not only do the frights come from nowhere, but they last a lot longer than a simple "Boo!"

The main misconception about anxiety isn't about how it feels, but rather how it looks. Like most mental illnesses, anxiety can take many forms, but it is widely known for trembling and shallow breathing. What do you think about when you hear the phrase *anxiety attack*? Hyperventilation? Nail-biting? Rocking back and forth on the floor of Panera Bread while humming the Nationwide jingle? You're not wrong, but there's more to anxiety than meets the eye, literally.

I was fourteen when I had my first panic attack. I was at school, asleep in a dorm with five other girls. There was nothing unusual about the days leading up to the attack. I had the same stresses most fourteen-year-old girls had at the time—crushes, homework, and Justin Timberlake leaving Janet Jackson out to dry for the Super Bowl halftime show "wardrobe malfunction." Standard stresses. There was nothing strange about that night either. Once in bed, we began our evening ritual of gossiping loudly, which quickly turned into gossiping quietly, which slowly petered out and ended with a soft, "Anyway, that's . . . what . . . I . . . heard." And the room fell silent.

The next thing I remember is my chest. I woke up and all I could think was "MY CHEST!" It felt like an elephant was sitting on my sternum. My rib cage started to (figuratively) cave in on itself, and I couldn't breathe. I was dry drowning, helplessly gulping at a room full of air while tears streamed down my face. There wasn't time to stop and think, "What the fuck is happening?" Other than getting my period, this was the only other time I'd experienced such an aggressive physical manifestation of anything, but this was a smidge more terrifying. All I could think about was making it stop. I furiously clawed at my chest in an attempt to rip through the skin and hold back my ribs. I just wanted oxygen by any means possible. The intensity with which I strained for air made me so dizzy I thought I was going to throw up. The skin on my face felt tight, like it was being pulled back. My head throbbed with the sound of my thudding heartbeat.

I could feel someone's hands on me. Their voice started off underwater but soon became clear. They were telling me to breathe, and I was like "YEAH, OK, GOOD IDEA." My body loosened while I reestablished breathing through traditional means, a.k.a. through my nose and mouth. There was some commotion as one of the senior girls went to find our house mistress, but I didn't pay attention. All I could do was lie there in shock and slight embarrassment. I couldn't understand what had happened. I felt betrayed by my body. I stared into nothing while the house mistress asked if I was ok. I nodded. It had lasted around fifteen, maybe twenty minutes from start to finish. I spent the rest of the night silently crying, thinking about what had happened and wondering if and when it would happen again.

Over the years, my bouts of anxiety have diversified. There have been instances when I've had a demonstrable attack, similar to my first. In my late twenties I experienced a rash of them that left the skin on my chest red and raw from where I'd raked at it for air. You never get used to anxiety. It's not something that gets easier over time, because every time it happens (and this may sound dramatic) you think you're going to die. Ok, maybe not *every* time. It's more like Russian roulette, only without the glamor.

To put it mildly, having these very visible attacks sucks. But nothing prepared me for the other end of anxiety—the tacit attacks. The ones where no one can tell what's going on because you're quietly freaking out. But there's nothing quiet about it in your mind. Imagine all the sensations I described in the previous paragraphs, but everything happens on the inside. It's like in cartoons when a character swallows a live grenade, causing their stomach to balloon from the explosion. (Cartoons are still like that, right?)

Some of the worst outbursts of anxiety I've experienced have been inbursts. I've had full-on panic attacks at parties, dinners, meetings, on public transport, in parks both national and regional—

honestly, just name a place and I've probably had an anxiety attack there.

We've talked about how anxiety can come from nowhere for no reason, but sometimes it can build slowly for a multitude of reasons. The moment I'm invited to a social event I start to feel it. As soon as I watch myself type "I'm in!" I'm already out. The back of my neck starts to burn up as my mind whirrs with thoughts of "How the hell are we going to get out of this one?" I shake it off. It's Future Amanda's problem; she'll think of something. It's a few days before, and I receive the not-so-gentle gentle reminder that the event is coming up and am I still coming? "You bet your ass I'm still coming!" Fuck, fuck, fuck. WHY, GOD, WHY? It's one of the cruel aspects of having anxiety: the more I freak out, the more adamant I am in confirming my attendance.

Later in the book I discuss the many excuses I dream up in order to avoid going to anything, but for now let's imagine I go. It's the big day, and I'm sweating from face to crack. I play the entire night in my head like a TV crime reenactment. I think about talking to people using words with my mouth hole and listening to other people say words from their mouth holes, and I ruminate on how much better it would be if I could stay at home with all my holes closed. I go to the event thinking it can't be as bad as I've made it out to be. Maybe I'm overreacting? Nope, it's just another callous trick anxiety can play on you: making you think you're a drama queen. You're not. You have anxiety. It's real and serious. That may sound obvious now, but in the moment you scramble to justify why you're like this and why can't you just be like everyone else? You look around and see people smiling, laughing, making talk so small you want to throw yourself into oncoming traffic. And guess what? Maybe they have anxiety too. You catch your reflection in a shiny surface and see that you're also smiling and laughing.

I've smiled, laughed, conversed, and been an overall joy to be around all while having a panic attack.

I used to write for an amazing sketch comedy company called Killing My Lobster who put on live shows every month in downtown San Francisco. It was my dream come true: writing comedy and working with super talented, funny people. After each show, we'd spill out into the bar area where friends and strangers would rave about the sketches. Now, I've never been one to shy away from a compliment, quite the opposite, I regularly try to steer into compliments any chance I get because validation from others is what keeps me alive. So why was this killing me?

I'm surrounded by people who I, for the most part, like, but grenades are detonating in my stomach. As they talk, I scream. An internal primal scream. My heart feels like it was being chased. Breath is a luxury I can afford only in installments. I inhale sharply through my nose and hold it until I felt confident enough to take in another. This all happens without the other person's knowledge. On the outside I was Amanda the Talking Human; on the inside I was "OH GOD NO." I say "was"—still am. Anxiety doesn't just rear itself during scary or sad moments, it can crop up at any time, even when you're happy, even during a moment you've waited for your whole life. Anxiety can happen anytime, anywhere, and look like nothing at all. Medication helps for the outwardly physical reactions, but I can't be knocking myself out with Ativan every time I'm at a "casual drinks thing" (although, let me tell you, I'd absolutely love to).

It's not just social events with loads of people that make me break out in hives. A simple one-on-one meeting can give me anxiety diarrhea. Everyone dreads those awful coffee dates where someone wants to "pick your brain." At best, they're awkward; at worst, they make you homicidal. There's not one part that's remotely enjoyable. If you get there first, you're the one tasked with finding a table with two free chairs (no mean feat!). Also, if you are the first, chances are you'll be on the receiving end of the "Running 5 mins late! Sorry!" text, further confirming your suspicion that this person is human garbage. By the time they burst through the door in a flurry of "Oh my god, traffic is crazy!" your coffee is cold and your desire to live is hanging by a thread. If you arrive on time and the person you're meant to meet is already there, it makes you question what their deal is and further confirms your suspicion that they're human garbage. You go to greet them, but you have to do that weird half-greet thing because now you have to get in line for coffee. So you set your stuff down on the chair and wait in line while you feel the other person watching you. All of this happens BEFORE THE MEETING BEGINS. It's natural to feel awkward when meeting people one-on-one. It doesn't mean you have an anxiety disorder, it just means you're human. And if you don't feel awkward, then you're a sociopath—it's called science.

For those of us who have an anxiety disorder, this stuff is more than an unpleasant and/or inconvenient waste of time; it's an all-consuming fog of tension. And it doesn't end when the meeting is over, oh no. We'll replay what was said on a loop for months. We'll overanalyze every word and gesture. We fantasize about what the other person must have thought of us. Not sexy fantasies like where a beautiful stranger consensually ravishes you in a back alley. Horrifying fantasies, like watching your parents do it on a futon.

Anxiety is tireless and often unpredictable. But there's one specific period of time when I guarantee I'll experience it: night time.

The Dark Night is when anxiety really comes into its own. The conditions are perfect; it's dark, quiet, no distractions. Throw in damp and you also have the perfect conditions for growing mold.

When you have a mental illness, there's nothing more terrifying than time alone with your thoughts. I know that meditation works for some people, but for me it's like waving to an assassin who's been hired to kill you and being all "Yoo hoo! Over here!"

The night is when anxiety transforms into a nightmarish radio station playing *DJ voice* your worst fears from the eighties, nineties, noughties, and today! Every thought, from the harrowing to the inconsequential, is now free to whip round your head uninterrupted. Until I took medication, this was my evening ritual. Sometimes I'd spin out into a physical panic attack, but more often than not I'd lie still in bed and quietly freak out. The only thing I could do was turn the light on. Once I turned on the light, I was able to focus a little better. Something about the darkness fed the anxiety and turbocharged the unsettling thoughts, OR I'm just a grown-ass woman who's still afraid of the dark. And I think we all know which one it is.

Wouldn't it be cool if right about now I shared some awesome breathing and mindfulness techniques that would help quell the hellfire of anxiety? What a nice little bow to stick on the end of this chapter. I could copy and paste some tips from *Psychology Journal* dot-com and call it a day. Tempting, but no.

The only thing that brings me any respite is medication. I know that's not the most uplifting answer, but it's the truth. Again, this is JUST ME and MY EXPERIENCE. Please do not DM me ranting about how the Headspace app helped you. I'm happy for you. But just because we're in the same boat doesn't mean we have to row the same way. Do whatever works for you and I'll do the same.

Trauma, Trauma, Trauma

For a long time, I thought PTSD was a condition you developed only after you fought in a war. And given that I'd never seen combat in my life, there was no way I could have it. In my mind, trauma was for serious stuff, such as war, extreme poverty, incarceration, and general violence. All my issues seemed trivial in comparison, like "Kim, there's people that are dying" trivial. I didn't believe I could have PTSD because . . . well, what trauma could I possibly have? A privileged, middle-class biracial girl who received a good education and grew up to be a satisfactory adult. This wasn't trauma; this was bellyaching!

When I started to experience horrific flashbacks of my brother's funeral, my abortion at nineteen, and, eventually, my suicide attempts, I assumed it was good ol' stress. But the thing with stress is it's often rooted in something universal, and most people can relate to it. If you're feeling overwhelmed at work or in your relationships, or if you have too much going on or not enough going on, people can empathize with that. PTSD stems from a specific event, a lived experience unique to you. It's not one of those things you can bring up at a dinner party and expect people to nod and say, "Been there, my friend!" Because this is somewhere only you know. It can't be brushed off or placed on the general stress pile. It's a distinct moment in time that can't be categorized, and because of that it sticks with you—not just as a feeling, but as a full-body experience.

That's the thing about PTSD: you don't just remember, you relive. I liken it to the scene at the end of *Ratatouille* in which the food critic, Anton Ego, tastes the ratatouille and is immediately whisked back to his childhood. His mother makes him ratatouille, and he remembers what it's like to feel happy. It's exactly like that, only without any of the happiness or ratatouille.

Even when I'm not in the throes of reliving traumatic memories, my PTSD still has ways of making itself known when I'm alone and free from distraction. So in the shower, I will involuntarily reprimand myself out loud. I don't want to say it's like Tourette's, because I hate when people do that with illnesses, but it's . . . kinda like Tourette's. Here's what happens. I'm in the shower, washing my bits, my mind is wide open, and I sense the trauma ready to pounce. Before it can take over, I'll shout, "Fuck you!" or "Kill yourself!"

This can go on for a few minutes or for the duration of the shower. Is it always "fuck you" and "kill yourself"? Great question. For the most part, yes. Other times I'll make an incoherent noise, like a mix between a meow and a scream. But why? Going straight for the jugular, I respect that. The honest answer is I don't know. I assume these little yelps of self-hate are my mind's way of defending itself from experiencing flashbacks, like Hadouken but for trauma. That's right, the mind that's inflicting the PTSD is the same mind trying to protect me from it.

To this day I haven't found a medication that can quiet these reflexes, and that's ok. As long as I'm not hurting myself or others, I'll take it. So if you see me muttering to myself, there's nothing to worry about. I'm not crazy; I'm just *very* crazy.

Trauma is physical. It lives in your bones. It's not "all in your head"; it's as much a part of you as any organ in your body. It's memory muscle. Your mind remembers what the trauma looks like, and your body recalls how it feels.

My brother was the happiest, most loving little boy. He called me Ga Ga because he couldn't pronounce Ga Jie (*sister* in Cantonese) yet. His warmth and laughter were contagious. I'm not exaggerating when I say this kid was always happy. He rarely cried and was astonishingly selfless for someone so young. He didn't need to be entertained 24/7. He was just content to be around people. One of my fondest memories is of him sitting on my bed, playing with my stuffed animals, and telling me how much he loved me. I'd blow raspberries on his spongy cheeks and tell him I loved him too. But the best feeling in the world was when he held my hand. I loved the feel of his doughy, often sticky, little hand in mine. He gripped me. He loved me. He made me better.

When he passed away, I didn't believe it. I cried for forever then shut down completely. Everyone told me I had to "stay strong" for the family, which is a huge ask for a teenager whose brother has just died. When you tell someone who's grieving or going through a rough time to "stay strong" for others, you're essentially telling them to lock up their feelings and cut their grief off. I know it sounds extreme and it's never anyone's intention, but phrases like "stay strong" or anything that encourages someone to "put on a brave face" can have damaging, lasting effects. JUST LOOK AT ME.

The only moments I remember from the funeral are the ones that continue to live inside me. I can vaguely recollect a religious building, possibly a church? And a service where, apparently, I sang "Amazing Grace" and read a poem I wrote for him. If I squint, I can see his tiny coffin sliding into the fiery mouth of a furnace, and the face of the EMT asking me if I was ok after I passed out from seeing his tiny coffin sliding into the fiery mouth of a furnace. But there is one memory I can recall in such vivid detail that if I close my eyes, I'm there.

I'm standing outside the church before the service. No one else is there yet. I'm told I can go see him one last time. It's a standard church—wooden pews, vaulted ceilings, stained glass, pulpits. The first thing I notice is that this church sanctuary is long. I look down at my feet and follow a red carpet that leads all the way to the altar. My eyes gaze steadily at the altar, giving themselves a second before they have to see him. I walk slowly down the carpet, and when I finally reach him, I'm relieved. He's not dead at all. He's sleeping! He's just been asleep this whole time! I know the difference between death and sleep; I've watched him sleep countless times. I look at his peaceful face, his cheeks still plump and rosy, and even though he's not smiling he still looks happy. He's always happy! But as serene as he looks right now, it's time to wake up, sleepyhead, time to go home. I reach into the casket to grab his doughy, often sticky, hand. The hand I've grabbed a thousand times before, during breakfast and cartoons, at the park and the mall. The hand I'd pretend to bite that he'd quickly withdraw as he squealed with laughter. The hand I held while he fell asleep. I grabbed it for the 1,001st time. It was cold and hard, like marble. My mind began to reel. What the fuck was going on? His hand isn't meant to feel like this. His hand is meant to be soft and warm. I reach out to pinch his cheeks. Marble. Like a statue. No. No. NO. I grip the sides of his casket, and I'm screaming, "YOU HAVE TO WAKE UP NOW! WE HAVE TO GO HOME!" But he's not waking up, and that's when I realize that my brother is dead. I don't know whose, but a man's hands are on my shoulders pulling me away. I try to fight him off, but my body gives out. I sob uncontrollably as I'm walked backward out of the church.

This was the last time I saw my brother "in the flesh." But in the sixteen years since, I've seen him, specifically this memory of him, hundreds of thousands of times.

My brother's funeral was not extraordinary, far from it. Everyone has experienced death, and most people have attended funerals. Trauma is more about how we experience exceptionally specific and painful moments that stem from seemingly ordinary events. These moments bury themselves in our subconscious, where they grow into trauma and sprout whenever they see fit.

Just like with all mental illnesses, there is no standardized trauma. There's no right or wrong way to experience it, and it certainly doesn't have one look or feel. Trauma is deeply personal, and while you may find someone who's been through something similar, your trauma is your own.

I still live with PTSD every day. Some days are better than others, but on the whole, it's steady. The only thing I've found that helps is—you guessed it—talking. I know, it's easier said than done. It took me years to even acknowledge my trauma, let alone talk about it. And even when I did talk about it, it was slow and staggered. I'd drip-feed morsels of information to my therapist, then stop and not revisit the topic for months.

I've been with my therapist for six years, and I still can't talk about my brother.

If experiencing trauma feels like being punctured by thousands of sharp metal objects, then talking about trauma feels like removing them, slowly, one by one. It's excruciating, but at least you don't have metal in your flesh anymore . . . yay?

If you're uncomfortable with the idea of talking or are unable to talk to someone, then that's ok. The important thing is finding a safe and healthy outlet. Whether it's writing, painting, vision boards—anything you can do to let it out will help. Trauma thrives in the darkness. Do what you can to bring it to light.

Good Will Hunting
Your Therapist

I'm very lucky and privileged to have a therapist. She's a psychiatrist, but I prefer the term *therapist* as it sounds a little . . . calmer? I dunno. Anyway, I didn't find Liz* in the traditional way. In fact, I've never known how to find a therapist. It's a question I get asked a lot, and I still don't have a good answer. There are a million online resources and, of course, the hellscape that is Yelp. But there's not one holy grail-esque place or site where you can go and find a therapist who is a good fit for you specifically. Therapy should be free and easy to access, because, if anything, it's cruel to make a depressed person do admin. Getting a therapist should be as easy as ordering shit-I-don't-need online—sort by rating, price, race, LGBTQ+ friendly, gender, add to cart, done. And just like ordering shit-I-don't-need online, it should be even easier to do while drunk or high, the true test of a great purchasing funnel.

I didn't find Liz; she found me, in a psych ward, which is not an ideal way of finding a therapist. But I've been with her ever since. Until then, my only experience with therapy had been with child psychiatrists, and that did not go well. I found them to be condescending, boring, and a waste of my precious time, because I was soooo busy at age nine.

A few years later, my feelings on psychiatrists changed because MOVIES. Movies made psychiatry look cool and dangerous, and the people who needed psychiatrists also looked cool and dangerous. But there was one movie, nay, one actor, who ruined psychiatrists for me: the brilliant Robin Williams in *Good Will Hunting*. For those who haven't seen it and can't be bothered to Wikipedia right now:

> Will Hunting has a genius-level IQ but chooses to work as a
> janitor at MIT. When he solves a difficult graduate-level math
> problem, his talents are discovered by Professor Gerald Lambeau,
> who decides to help the misguided youth reach his potential.
> When Will is arrested for attacking a police officer, Professor
> Lambeau makes a deal to get leniency for him if he will get treat-
> ment from therapist Sean Maguire (Robin Williams).

Sean Maguire was at once no-nonsense and empathetic. He cared about his clients on a level I'd never seen before. He became a father figure to Will. And as much as Will tried to push him away, Maguire wouldn't let him. He stood by Will when everyone else abandoned him. There's one famous scene where they're in session and Maguire tells Will, "It's not your fault." At first Will is all "Nah, you're good," but Maguire pushes on and repeats, "It's not your fault." This goes on for a while, and yada yada yada, they end up hugging and crying. I remember watching that scene and thinking, "If this is what psychiatrists are like, then count me in!"

Fast-forward sixteen years. I'd done my stints in a psych ward and psychiatric hospital. I'd spoken to many psychiatrists, thera-pists, nurses, and doctors along the way. I was done being crazy. I was done talking. I was done.

Turns out, I was not done, because now I'm sitting opposite Liz in her office, and I'm mad.

I don't want to be here. I have friends, a boyfriend, and other shit to do. I don't have time for this.

Liz asks questions. I shrug. I'm exasperated and want to scream, "I've been through this a million times already! Can't you just look at my chart?" We sit in silence. For the first time since I walked in, I take a good look at Liz, a tiny white lady in her late fifties or early sixties. She has a stern, dark bob that frames her sweet, doll-like face. Her voice is soft and contains flecks of Minnesotan. But I'm not listening. I'm indignant. Why do I have to speak to this stranger when I'm fixed?

Liz broke the silence with another question. I gave some belligerent non-answer because I'm a spoiled, mentally ill brat, and we wait it out until "that's time." Needless to say, the first session was not a success. In fact, the first thirty weren't successes. It would take nearly a year before I felt any progress or experienced any (what movies like to call) "breakthroughs."

All this time, I thought therapy was going to be dramatic (*Good Will Hunting*), suspenseful (*The Silence of the Lambs*), and mildly amusing (*Analyze This*). But it was none of those things, although it is a lot funnier than *Analyze This*. And while I'm glad and grateful to have a therapist, it took me a while to fully appreciate therapy for what it is. Here are a few things I've learned in the past five years.

Therapy is hard fucking work.

You can't just go to therapy for three months and be like, "I'm good now." Therapy takes time, and in order for it to really work, you have to be consistent with your attendance. Which is particularly cruel, because the two things people don't have a lot of these days are time and money. Thankfully there are more affordable resources popping up all the time, but it's still not ideal. We should be up to our nose hairs in accessible therapy options. Aside from time and money, there's the searching and the waiting. There are people *with* insurance who have to wait months to see a therapist, so just think of those without. It's fucked, but you already knew that. And me ranting about the broken American healthcare system isn't going to solve anything, but if it does then please credit me and me alone. Honestly a Pulitzer is fine. Anyway, if you are able to talk to someone on a weekly or monthly basis, stick to it. Show up like it's your job (assuming your job is important to you). The "work" doesn't get easier. But the more you go, the more tools you'll acquire, and *that* is what will make the work easier. It's not a case of "practice makes perfect"—more like "practice makes progress."

Therapy is strange. You sit in a room with a stranger and tell them your deepest, darkest thoughts and feelings. At first, it seems downright unnatural to just talk about yourself for forty-five minutes. There's a lot of stopping and starting. You're careful and guarded about what you say because of course you are! This person is a stranger! But you get yourself into a flow, and one day there's more starting than stopping. You find yourself sharing a little more each time. And although what you're sharing may not always feel good at the time, it will pay off later—trust me. I know it's cheesy when people say therapy is an investment in yourself, so I'll say it. Therapy is an investment in yourself.

Put the work in. There will be days when you feel like total shit, or you can't be bothered, or think you're "cured," but that's how you got here in the first place. At least that's how I did. It will suck. Then it will be good. Then it will suck again. When it comes to your mind, there's no quick and easy fix. You won't be "cured" but, little by little, you will heal. It may not feel like that now, it may not feel like that in three months, but one day it will. And trust me, that one day is worth the wait.

Your therapist won't tell you what to do, and it's infuriating.

I know! If therapists won't tell you what choices to make or how to live your life, then what is the point? There have been so many times when I've asked Liz, "What should I do?" and she comes back with variations on, "What do you feel like you should do?" And it makes me want to throw all her *DSM-5*s out the window. It feels like some bullshit deflection or an infurtiating game of hide-and-seek in which your therapist has hidden the answers. It's almost as if they want us to do their jobs for them! And they kinda do. At the risk of sounding like a Pinterest quote, therapists don't give us the answer; they help us get there. AND IT SUCKS. I *want* to be told what to do. Not just in therapy, but in all aspects of my life. I want to be told what to eat, how to dress, and if I should join that fancy expensive women-only co-working space even though I can't afford it, but, like I could write this book there plus they have showers.

When you're someone who feels hopeless and depressed most of the time, you don't want to have to work things out. Not because you're lazy but because in order to make any decision, you must first complete an obstacle course set in the foggy forest of your mind. It's exhausting. Everything is a chore. Living is a chore. Chores become double chores, it's chore-ception. But you know who isn't exhausted (at least in your mind they're not)? Your therapist. Plus, they've seen it all! If there's one person equipped to tell you what to do, it's them. Then why won't they? To keep us coming back? That's what Big Therapy wants, comrades!

The answer is less dramatic than that. It's simply all part of "the work." It's about giving you space and time to think it through rather than automatically being fed an answer. And the reason I hate it so much is because thinking is scary. Historically, "thinking" hasn't worked out too well for me. But when I'm forced to think out loud, in a safe environment with a mental health professional, it allows me to unknot my unhealthy, tired, and often dangerous thinking. It's tiring but not like doing chores because I know doing "the work" will strengthen my mind but doing chores will always be bullshit.

It's trains you to be a little more mentally independent which is good because you don't want to become reliant on someone else's opinion for every part of your life. If so, you might as well steal their identity and start anew. Is that what you want? To *be* your therapist? Of course not! You'd have to see and talk to people like *us* every day, which, no offense to us, would be my personal hell . If you're in therapy, chances are you've spent most of your life wrapped up in depression, trauma, or some other condition that's stopped you from being you. This is a chance to unwrap yourself. At the risk of sounding like an e-card you receive from an aunt, there's only one person who can answer your questions, and that's you.

And if you thought that I've learned to stop asking Liz to tell me what to do, then thank you for overestimating me. After all these years, through the depression, trauma, and suicides, she has only ONCE ever told me what to do – don't join the women-only co-working space. No showers for me then.

Therapy is a lot like sex in that you wonder how everyone else does it.

I always wonder if I'm doing therapy "right." I often find myself thinking about what other people do with their therapists. What about Liz's other patients? How do they do it? Does Liz have more fun with them? Are these the best questions to be asking while I'm in session?

Here's a rundown of how my sessions go: I used to sit on a chair. When I got a little more comfortable (three years later), I graduated to sitting on the couch. Liz will ask me how I am, and I'll say either "ok" (a.k.a. eh), "not great" (a.k.a. bad), or "not good" (a.k.a. I'm hanging by a tiny thread). She'll ask me why, and that's how it all starts. I'll talk, and she'll listen. Sometimes she asks questions; other times she'll offer her insight and thoughts. All therapists are different. But when it comes down to it, you're having a conversation, which is hard to get wrong. It used to take me a while to get going, even after I got over the whole sharing-your-darkness-with-a-stranger barrier. I started to doubt whether my issues were worthy enough for therapy. Was my life harrowing enough? And how did it stack up against everyone else's? That's right, I was secretly competing with Liz's other patients for World's Worst Trauma, which is 100 percent insane and thus therapy worthy.

I don't cry that much in therapy, which worries me, because it seems like a common by-product of therapy. Don't get me wrong, I cry a lot in all other situations. The shower, the street, at work, silently in a Library, or loudly just outside the Library—the world is my crying oyster. I don't know why I'm not a big therapy crier. I suspect it has something to do with the intense one-on-one setup. To me, it feels more natural, acceptable even, to cry in front of Joanna Gaines's rustic throw pillows in the home furnishings section of Target than it does directly in front of one person. But what I lack in crying, I more than make up for in other behaviors borne out of deep trauma. I went through a phase of crawling under Liz's furniture. I would become so overwhelmed by the unpacking of feelings that I'd fall to the floor and roll myself under the coffee table. My body needed a small, cave-like space in which to unravel. Once there, I'd convulse, scream, and babble incoherently for the rest of the session. Liz would try to coax me out, but for the most part she'd let me lie there and do what I needed to do. And even though I don't crawl under the table anymore, I do curl up and try to find a small, dark space, whenever I revisit trauma. Again, I'm not fixed, I'm just not under the table.

There is no right way to do therapy. It's what you make of it. Whether it's sitting in silence or bawling your eyes out, it's all about you and what you need. Try not to think about what your therapist thinks (they've seen worse), and try not to think about how other people are doing it (focus that energy on how other people are doing sex).

It doesn't always make you feel better, but it won't make you feel worse either!

I assumed I'd leave every session feeling light and free, the same way it feels to unload a heavy backpack or take a huge dump. I imagined I'd walk out into the sunshine, eyes closed with elation, ready to LIVE, just like Nicole Kidman leaving her lawyer's office after her divorce from Tom Cruise was finalized.

To be fair, most of the time I do feel relief upon leaving therapy. I'm a true believer in "a problem shared is a problem halved." But don't be shocked if, on occasion, you leave therapy feeling less than good.

In the early days (I'm five years in and it still feels like the early days, but whatever), I came out of sessions feeling confused more than anything. I wasn't used to talking about myself so much. Not true—I'm pretty self-centered. I just wasn't used to talking about my mental state. I had to start from scratch with my mind, which seemed both absurd and impossible, like trying to disassemble Mount Everest. There were times when I'd leave with more questions than answers. I'd get home and feel out of sorts. I'd replay the session in my head in an attempt to understand what I'd said and why I'd said it. I thought therapy was where you could unload and leave your thoughts, like a thought day care. So why was I leaving with *more* feelings? What a fucking scam!

I was drowning in trauma both old and new. Looking back, I should have (1) talked about it with Liz and (2) given myself time to process those additional feelings. I didn't do either, and as a result I ended up in the hospital for the second time. I was so hell-bent on "fixing" myself as fast as possible. Instead of taking the time to climb the mountain, I decided to drill right through it.

I wanted to give up. I wanted a fast pass through therapy. I was tired of sorting through a pile of shit only to find another one pop up in its place.

It was only when I woke up from my second suicide attempt that I realized I couldn't "power through" my mental illness. I needed to take the time to sit in it, confront it, and get to know it. It's something I continue to battle with/work on every day. I know it hurts, and I know you're tired, but keep going. It'll be worth it. I'll see you on the other side. Where there's another mountain, but it's ok. You've got this.

There are no breakthroughs.

Ok, that's misleading. Many people experience breakthroughs in therapy, but they're not always as melodramatic as movies would have you believe. First of all, I expected to have *at least* one break-through a week, each more profound than the last. I imagined putting my head in my hands, bursting into tears, and sobbing, "You're right, you're so right." And as my self-actualizations gushed forth, I'd reach for tissue after tissue, before finally flopping onto a chaise longue in a satisfied daze of my own progress. I needed my breakthroughs to be deep, insightful, but, above all, filled with theatrics. I've experienced movie-worthy breakthroughs only a couple of times, and while they were extravagant and everything I dreamed they would be, my most meaningful discoveries were quiet and reflective.

When it eventually dawned on me that I needed to cut certain family members out of my life, there were no tears, no fears, no dropping to my knees and screaming "WHYYYY" into the sky. I just sat there and took it in, like a majestic sunset or an anal suppository. And despite the lack of mental fireworks, I felt at peace. But I wasn't done yet. It took a few more days to process my thoughts, a few more sessions to crystallize my plan, and a few more months before I could act on it. Breakthroughs come in all shapes and sizes. It doesn't matter *how* you experience them; the important thing is how you can learn from them.

Therapy can be boring.

Sometimes you won't have anything new to say, and that's ok. Therapy doesn't have to be filled with heartbreak or sadness every session. I often considered making up some harrowing shit just so Liz wouldn't think I was wasting her time. I know it sounds messed up but, yeah. I don't have an excuse.

Truth be told, I've never fabricated anything in therapy. On the days I don't feel like getting into the doom and gloom, I do the opposite—I gossip.

I gossip about friends, celebs, neighbors, because chatting shit feels GOOD, especially when you have that sweet patient confidentiality. And for those who think I'm wasting precious therapy time, let me remind you that (1) you're absolutely right and (2) it's not a waste at all. If you're someone who has a mental illness—or even if you don't, but you feel low and a little isolated—any time you talk, IT HELPS. It doesn't matter what you're talking about. The fact that you're sharing and connecting with another human being is enough and (3) you're right though.

It is very hard to make a therapist cry. Trust me, I've tried.

It's my holy grail. If you've ever achieved this, I'd love to know how. I must break Liz before I die.

If all else fails—Dreams.

Therapists fucking love dreams. Especially dreams involving family members. The happiest I've ever seen Liz is when I told her I had a dream about my father. One time she literally RUBBED HER HANDS TOGETHER like some sort of goddamn Disney villain at the thought of me talking about a dream. If you have a dream where you kill or fuck a relative, tell your therapist; it'll make their day. It may even make them cry.

PART 3
Medication

Medication, Medication, Medication

A few things I want to make clear from the jump:

- Medication saved my life.
- Medication works for some people and not others.
- If meds work for you, take them.
- This is *my* experience with meds, which will be different from yours.

I just wanted to put that up top in case someone didn't feel like reading the rest of the chapter.

I was never against medication prediagnosis. I was always down to take antibiotics, painkillers, and antihistamines; they're normal meds for normal people. No one bats an eyelid when you pop a Tylenol or chug down some Robitussin. When it comes to physical pain with physical symptoms, people roll out the med carpet. Headaches are a prime example of this. All you need to do is rub your temples, and suddenly everyone's rummaging in their bags for ibuprofen. Someone once offered me codeine for a headache, which may seem like overkill, but let me tell you—it was, and I loved it. My headache vanished almost instantly, my body felt lined with warmth, and I started to sing "Pure Imagination" from *Willy Wonka and the Chocolate Factory* (1971). Good times.

Postdiagnosis is a different story.

The first time I was prescribed *medication* was in the psychiatric hospital. The head psychiatrist reeled off a grocery list of antidepressants and antipsychotics on which they were going to start me. He discussed their effects and side effects, both of which were terrifying. But the thing that stood out were the names. They didn't sound like powerful mind-altering medications, but rather like whimsical Shakespearean heroines:

Abilify

- Soft, delicate, can be shortened to Abbi.
- "Come hither, Abilify, and help mother with the horses."
- Used for schizophrenia, bipolar disorder, and depression.

Latuda

- Strong, confident, can be shortened to Lats.
- "Now then, young Latuda, have you been frolicking in the moors again?"
- Used for bipolar disorder and schizophrenia.

Saphris

- Elegant, regal, can be shortened to Saffy.
- "Listen here, Saphris, I forbid you from seeing that Latuda in the moors!"
- Used for treatment of manic and mixed bipolar episodes.

It seemed as though the list was never-ending. I tried to take in as much information as possible, but all I could think was, "Fuck, I'm, like, properly mental." I'd turned into one of those people who needed "crazy pills." I asked how long I needed to be on all these meds, and the answer was simply, "We'll see."

I'd line up every morning to receive my tiny paper cup filled with a mix of Shakespearean heroines and down it like a shot of wheatgrass. Yeah, I like wheatgrass; bet you didn't see that coming (neither did I). After about an hour, I felt 100 percent better and was told I could go home . . . is what I would love to tell you, but obviously not.

People think popping a pill can change everything in an instant, and why wouldn't they? There are pills that cure headaches, allergies, and diarrhea within minutes. If a pill can stop a torrent of shit from blasting out of my anus, then surely an antidepressant can make me happy, RIGHT?

I've admitted to having problematic thoughts on medication in the past. I believed they were prescribed to either dangerous psychos or miserable attention-seekers. I wasn't against meds; I was just against me being on them. I didn't want to be seen as a broken, mental person. I wanted to be normal, and being reliant on drugs was far from normal.

By the time I was admitted to the psychiatric hospital, it had become abundantly clear that I needed to be on medication, and I wasn't going to fight it. I'd accepted that these drugs were not solely for psychos or attention-seekers, but I had so much more to learn. I assumed that the meds I was assigned that first day were going to be my meds for the rest of time—same meds, same dosage, same frequency. But you know what they say: "Assumption is the mother of all things not going well."

Just because a qualified psychiatrist assigns you specific meds doesn't mean they're going to work from the get-go. In fact, it takes a long time, and a lot of heartbreak, to get your meds "right." This was something I had to learn the hard way. I'm a naturally impatient person, so the fact that the pills weren't working in a timely manner made me only more depressed.

In the hospital, I was on a rigorous routine of intensive therapy sessions (both group and individual) and medication. I was surrounded by professional and caring members of staff at all hours. And it didn't hurt that the hospital was nestled in the corner of a picturesque Bostonian woodland. After gulping down my morning pills, I'd put on every piece of clothing I had (this was Boston in the winter), strap on some snow boots, and head out for a thirty-minute walk. I'm not an outdoorsy person at all, but there was something about this walk that soothed me. The air was clean and frigid, which gave me a rosy, rash-looking situation. Trekking through the snowy woods among the towering, barren trees made me feel like an extra in a Tim Burton movie. It was peaceful yet eerie. I saw only two or three other humans while I was out there. I didn't recognize them from the hospital, so I presumed they were just outdoorsy weirdos who did this for fun rather than for running away from their mental disorders. By the time I'd return to the hospital, my face would be a flushed mess dripping with snot and wind tears, but I felt fantastic. But this isn't an uplifting story about how walking helped cure my bipolar. I spent the rest of the day in back-to-back therapy sessions. I was on strong medication in a controlled environment. And while it sounds idyllic, it wasn't real life; it was serious rehabilitation. My meds were working for me while I was on the "inside," but that was all about to change.

After I left the hospital, I was put on a strict outpatient schedule. I had two psychiatrists, one of whom was Liz. The other was a man we'll call "Tim." Tim was in charge of my medication, and Liz was my day-to-day therapist. There's a stark difference between being on meds in a woodland rehab and being on meds at work in an open plan office. Even though I had a routine in place, coming out of the hospital was a shock not unlike jumping from a sauna into an ice fishing hole. I had to dole out my own meds and make my own way to appointments. And on top of all that, I had to do real life.

The first day back, I was determined to "Make it work!" and "Have it all!" and other lies society tells women. The next few days were a blur. I was flying high on adrenaline and stress, and although I kept up with my therapist appointments and medication, everything else fell by the wayside. I was more focused on getting back to my "normal" life than I was on looking after myself. Seeing my friends again was awesome, but seeing the looks on their faces shook me. They looked at me like I was a three-legged puppy trying to climb a flight of stairs, with a mix of awww and pity. "Awww" I can handle, but pity? Being pitied is worse than being hated! I received a similar reaction when I went back to work, only it was less awww and more of a "don't give her anything important to do" kinda vibe. I'd spent weeks in a warm bubble where having a mental illness was the norm, where no one avoided the subject, and everyone was just, like, chill about it. I was naive to expect people in the real world to follow suit. Between work, friends, and a crumbling relationship, there was no time for my hospital schedule. I didn't have whole days dedicated to therapy anymore. I had to live!

All this mental health stuff felt like too much work, and a few weeks later my schedule fell apart. The only thing I stuck to religiously was taking my meds. I believed that medication, and medication alone, would solve everything. Also, popping pills didn't eat into my precious social time, which ranked high on my list of "Things Worth Doing for My Mental State."

This strategy lasted a grand total of one more week, when it became clear I was heavily undermedicated. What I thought was adrenaline and stress was really hypomania. The combination of desperately wanting to be normal and weak levels of meds sent me into a weeklong manic state. I thought I was "making up for lost time" with my friends, when really I was shouting and sweating at them. I could feel my mind tearing at the seams, but I couldn't work out why. You can't be crazy if you take your meds. IT'S SCIENCE! Turns out, you very much can. What had worked for me in the hospital was not working for me on the outside. Tim and I discussed making some adjustments to the dosages and maybe introducing a couple of new drugs to help keep me intact. At first, it was a relief. The whole hypomanic state was merely a blip, a bud that we very quickly nipped. Now I could go forth and be normal, which is exactly what I did, and everything worked out perfectly. Wouldn't that be a great way to end a chapter?

Anyway, I'd been on my new med regimen for a month when it became clear that I was now heavily *over*medicated. I found it so hard to stay awake during the day that I was falling asleep at my desk. I'd gained around ten pounds in a week and had taken to rolling everywhere as opposed to walking. I was like an adolescent zombie—moody, zoned out, and hungry for brains. Once again, I went back to Tim and was like, "You've got to be shitting me." How could a qualified psychiatrist fuck this up? TWICE? The frustrating answer is, it happens all the time.

The human mind is so complex and ever changing that trying to "fix" one part of it is like trying to play whack-a-mole with a toothpick and a million moles. When it comes to medication, there is no silver bullet, especially when you have a mood disorder. It's not just chemicals in your brain; it's your environment, your physical state, and also that thing someone said to you that one time. All of it affects your mood.

A headache, cough, or allergy can be located and dealt with swiftly because the pain or other symptom is rooted and often sticks to one spot. Mental illness, on the other hand, is a constant moving target. I still wake up every morning and think, "Am I gonna lose it today?"

I don't see Tim anymore. It's just Liz and me now. We've worked hard over the past few years to make sure my meds are in check, but by no means have we perfected the levels. We've fucked up a few times. More than a few. The best solution we have is to simply check in with each other about my regimen as often as we can. I know it sounds obvious, but once you get into a rhythm with therapy, you tend to forget to talk about medication, especially if you've been feeling "good" for a stretch of time. If I find myself slipping into a depressive or manic state, Liz and I will address my mental state and medication, because for me, it's not either-or. Again, that's what works for me.

I know people who've been on the same meds for years and have not needed to change a thing. I know people who take meds but don't see a therapist, and vice versa. And I know people who use crystals instead of medication, but that's a different chapter.

The first time I felt good on meds was a revelation. It felt like my mind could breathe. And when I say "good" I don't mean happy. I'm not happy at all. By "good" I mean in control and not completely helpless. I'd been at the mercy of my mind for so long that I'd forgotten what it was like to be in charge. The fog had dissolved and given way to a clarity I'd never known. I could make my own choices, I could do a chore, and for once I could hear myself think.

But don't be fooled by my hyperbolic praise of meds. Make no mistake: I still have depression. I still have suicidal ideation. And I still fight with my mind every day. The difference is it's more manageable. And that's the best any of us can hope for. So if you're struggling with medication, talk to your doctor or therapist (if you can). After that, the most important thing is to be patient. It'll take time, and it'll probably suck, but you'll get there.

Side Effects:
Label vs. Life

I can't very well write a whole section of the book about medication without giving you a list of meds I take and have taken, now can I?

Latuda

Antipsychotic. 40 mg.

I'd be dead without Latuda, but I'd also be a lot more alert. I don't want to shit on it, because it literally kept me sane, but it can dull your mind. Not in a major way. It just sometimes takes me a second to respond, and oftentimes that's not a bad thing. I don't take it at the moment but I want to be clear, LATUDA DOESN'T MAKE YOU DULL OR LESS CREATIVE OR ANY BULLSHIT LIKE THAT. It just levels you out. Maybe I shouldn't have used the word *dull*. Ugh. Great start.

Lithium

Prevents bipolar manic episodes. 900 mg.

Lithium is my main med. Whenever pharmacists hand me this prescription, I'm pretty sure they're like, "Oh, so you're *crazy* crazy." Obviously, they never say it, but I see you, pharmacist, I see you. Most people know what lithium is for. It's one of those old-school meds. Nirvana even had a song called "Lithium"—the one where the chorus is just "Yeah" fourteen times, which I feel perfectly captures the essence of the drug. I do well on lithium, except when I take it before bed. Then it gives me nightmares. No one is allowed to challenge me on this. I've run my tests. It also makes me want to piss all the time. I often wake up in the middle of the night to squeeze out a thimble of urine like I'm ninety. That said, lithium keeps my mind intact, and I'd keep taking it even if it made me wet my pants in public.

Citalopram

Antidepressant. 10 mg.

Soon after I started taking citalopram, I began having manic episodes. It tapped into my bipolar and amplified it real quick. Now, I'm usually an insecure, self-loathing mess, but on citalopram I AM A GOD OF GODS. It made me feel omniscient but also irritable and sweaty. My body overheated from mania while my brain overheated from delusions of grandeur. In my mind I was Gemma Chan, but in reality I was more like a raccoon strapped to a rocket.

I don't remember a lot from this period. I tend to black out during manic episodes. I know these details only because I asked my psychiatrist to go through my medical history with me for this chapter. Apparently, at one point I told her I had "energy searing through my blood!" Which I think sounds awesome. Needless to say, I don't take citalopram anymore.

Trazodone

Sedative/antidepressant. 100 mg.

I call trazodone "Traz" because I'm awful like that. I honestly don't know if it works for me or not. When you take more than three types of medication per day, it's hard to figure out what is doing what. I take Traz as a sedative, but it never keeps me down. Honest to god, I think my body is resistant to it. Over the years I've built up the boisterous tolerance of a wild thoroughbred. Team that with the high-speed thoughts of a paranoid meerkat and you have a . . . very weird animal.

Lorazepam
Treats anxiety. 1 mg.

I love lorazepam more than I love most people. It's the only drug that (for a short period) can extinguish the fire in my mind. It offers palpable relief, like putting aloe on a burn or being canceled on last minute. It's addictive. I crave its soothing abilities. The thing is, I often mistake "soothing relief" with "being knocked the fuck out," which is pretty dangerous. I also call it "Pam," which is unhealthy and irresponsible because it makes it sound sort of endearing, like a caring old lady. She'd make me soup, wrap me in a blanket, and then knock me the fuck out.

Saphris
Antipsychotic. 10 mg.

Saphris is the most intense medication I've ever taken. I used to take it before bed. Within minutes I would be dead to the world, which is saying something, given that no medication before or since has been able to take me down as quickly as Saphris. Then came the dreams. My god. It was like, before, my dreams were in black and white, but on Saphris, they were this 4-D, Technicolor, Dolby surround sound shit. I remember them to this day. I'm not going to describe them here because I'm not a monster. However, they did feel a lot like immersive theater, in that at first you're like, "Ok, not as bad as I thought it was going to be." Then you're like,

"Alright this is a little much." And eventually you're like, "WHY CAN'T I LEAVE? DOES ANYONE WORK HERE, OR ARE THEY ALL ACTORS? WTF?" In "normal" dreams, your body tends to wake you up right before or after something horrifying happens. On Saphris, you're made to experience your nightmare in full, no breaks.

Viibryd
Antidepressant. 10 mg.

Pretty sure Viibryd never worked for me. I remember taking it and still feeling super depressed (which is different from the "medium depression" I feel most days). Also, the name is kind of weird, even by medication standards. I kept calling it "Vye Bird," so maybe I was given a different drug instead? Maybe I was given "Vye Bird," which definitely sounds like a thrush medication aimed at millennial women. "Say Vye Vye Birdy to vaginal thrush!"

Hydroxyzine
Treats anxiety/nausea. 25 mg.

Hydroxyzine is like a confident Benadryl. It makes you so drowsy that you forget why you had anxiety in the first place. It won't put you to sleep, but it will turn you into a drunk baby for a bit.

Propranolol
Beta-blocker. 20 mg, 60 tablets.

I take propranolol for heart palpitations. I often take it before I have to go to a place where there will be people and things, or if I think about going to a place where there will be people and things. Does it work? Depends on the number of people and things.

Abilify

Antipsychotic. 10 mg.

When I think of Abilify, I think of one thing: weight gain. I'm talking weight gain that doesn't even have the decency to creep up on you. I gained, like, fifteen pounds in two weeks. The change was so fast that my mind had a hard time processing it. The weight gain made me more depressed, so I took more Abilify and gained more weight. It was fucking vicious.

Your Friends' Quick and Easy Cures

I wanted to take this time to discuss a pet peeve of mine: when people suggest cures for your mental illness. And this isn't something only mentally well people do. Oh no, even people who have mental illnesses will recommend alternative remedies to you! I say this is a pet peeve of *mine*, but I'm pretty sure it has happened to most people. If you've ever been in a conversation about mental health and you happen to mention you have depression, there's always someone on hand who's all "Have you tried exercising? It helps." Or if you've ever written anything online about your mental health, there's always a flood of comments giving you advice on how to handle your illness, in addition to those telling you to kill yourself. Good online times.

I realize the majority of these suggestions come from a good place, I do. However, what people have to understand is that this kind of behavior is incredibly harmful. By proffering up a "simple solution" like exercise, you're implying that this illness is "fixable." What you're also doing is assuming that this person has never heard of exercise, which is just plain insulting. Now, I'm sure all your little tricks worked for you or "someone" you know, but I'm going to assume you are not a mental health professional, and you do not know the ins and outs of this person's mental illness, so you shouldn't be doling out advice. The same goes for anything in life ever. If you are not qualified or if someone hasn't asked you for your opinion, the best thing you can do is shut the hell up.

It comes down to visibility. Mental illness is a largely invisible illness, which is one of the main reasons why it's so stigmatized, but it's also one of the main reasons why people feel like they can suggest any old crap to you. When the hurt is on the outside, no one can argue with it. When you see someone with a broken leg, you typically don't make a treatment suggestion. Most of the time people ask, "What did the doctor say?" Oh, so NOW you ask about the doctor?

It can be so infuriating—especially when it comes from your own kind! I've had people with depression give me "tips" on how to handle my depression, which would be cool if I asked for tips in the first place, but I don't.

You can't assume that just because something works for you means it'll work for me. You see, mental illness is like sex: everyone experiences it differently, and what turns you on probably won't turn me on. If I tell you I'm struggling to get off in the bedroom and you suggest that I become a Furry because animal costumes are a huge turn-on for you, that ain't gonna work. And while I'm happy that you've found your kink, I know it's not for me, even if I do find the cartoon fox in Disney's *Robin Hood* incredibly charming. He HAS CHARISMA.

The only time you should give anyone advice on their mental well-being is if they ASK for it.

I made up a term for people who love to cure other people's mental state: *curist*. Many mentally ill people have encountered curists at some point in their lives. And while curists come in all different shapes and sizes, in my experience they've mostly been white women in-person and white men online. People of color do talk about mental health online, but in my experience, it's mainly been white people giving out recommendations. It takes a particular brand of confidence to approach someone you barely know and inform them how they should be living their life.

Over the years, I've gotten used to this line of inquiry. I've even managed to develop some empathy for curists, but part of me is still irritated whenever I'm challenged on my mental illness. It's the part that screams inwardly, "You don't think I've tried this shit already?"

Now when I'm questioned by a curist, sometimes I nod politely and mumble, "Cool, yeah, I'll check that out," but most of the time I stay silent while astral projecting to a time and place where Keanu Reeves is riding his motorcycle through Big Sur and I'm the motorcycle.

Maybe there are some mentally ill people who appreciate the unsolicited advice. Maybe they're truly not bothered, or maybe they're less highly strung than I am. For me, it's hard enough trying to manage a mental illness without having literal strangers tell you how to do it better. I've had conversations with people I barely know that have gone like this:

Setting: A gathering of humans.

Me: So I was like, "I'm no surgeon, but I know that's not meant to be there!"

Uproarious laughter

Curist, weaving their way into the group: Amanda, hi, I'm Curist.

Me: Please no. Hello.

Curist: I couldn't help but overhear you say you're bipolar.

Me: Sure, you couldn't. Yes.

Curist: Awww, that's rough.

Me: It is.

Curist: You know I have a cousin who's bipolar.

Me: I did not.

Curist: Well, she was bipolar.

Me: ~~Oh, did she die?~~ Oh really?

Curist: Let me ask you something—have you tried chewing on
   licorice root?†

Me: ~~Keanu, these roads are so...winding . . .~~ I have not.

Curist: I know it sounds weird and you probably think I'm crazy—

Me: ~~Yes.~~

Curist: But I'm telling you, it really cleared up my cousin's bipolar.

Me: ~~Cleared up? Like acne?~~

Curist: She used to be up and down and up and down. Nothing
   helped. And, between you and me, I'm pretty sure those
   medications were making her worse.

Me: ~~To have and to hold, in sickness and in health . . .~~

Curist: Anyway, she read up on these homeopathic treatments—
   have you read about them? You should. And she found out
   about this licorice root, so she started chewing on it every day,
   and you'd never guess what happened.

Me: ~~I'm guessing you're going to tell me.~~

Curist: The bipolar subsided! She wasn't up and down anymore. It's
   been six months, and she's better than ever. It's like she never
   had it. Anyway, just thought you'd like to know.

Me: ~~I didn't.~~ Oh wow.

Curist: Thought maybe you'd wanna give it a go, seeing as you're
   still . . . you know . . . Think about it. *Pats me on the

shoulder.* It works. Trust me. My cousin. Cured. That could be you. Just a suggestion! Let me know how it goes.

Me: ~~I won't.~~ I will.

Curist: You are so welcome. *Bows.*

There are different ways to deal with curists. One way is to say, "I know you think you're helping, but you're not. I appreciate you trying, but I have my own ways of dealing with my stuff. If I want your advice, I'll be sure to ask for it. Now, who wants another drink?" For those looking for a less confrontational coping strategy: put yourself in their shoes. While they blabber on about some "technique" they learned about on some "retreat," think about *why* they're saying these things, and you'll soon realize that they're projecting. Curists are also grappling with their mental health; they just don't know it yet, poor lambs. Next time one of them launches into their list of "fixes," just know that they're mostly saying this stuff for their own sake, not for you.

If you're a curist reading this, you're probably gearing up to write me a strongly worded email or call me a bitch on Twitter. But know this: I'm not saying that what you do is wrong or dangerous (although it is absolutely both those things). I'm saying don't dish out hot nonsense unless someone explicitly asks for it. That said, if you are a curist, I'm going to take this time to satisfy all your agenda-pushing needs. I've created an FAQ that answers every question you have about how I'm managing my mental illnesses. Enjoy.

Have you tried eating healthy?

It's a little difficult to maintain a balanced diet when you want to die. You're either never hungry, always hungry, or grazing all day cow-style. I'd eat the weirdest combination of foods just because I'd see them. You ever opened the fridge and all you have is an open can of tuna, one lemon, and a carton of whipping cream? I have, and I ate it together in one sitting. When you're that numb and that low, it doesn't matter what you're eating, just as long as you're doing an activity that's not suicide. But, like, apart from that, yeah, I eat vegetables.

Have you tried exercising?

When I'm able to drag my unwashed body from my bed grave because my mind has kindly decided not to fight me on this particular day, then you betcha! I get most of my exercise from walking my dog and anxiety attacks,. Here's the thing: exercise doesn't help; *regular* exercise helps, and that's the problem. One time I exercised every day for two weeks. Was I hypomanic? Probably, but that's not the point. I felt great. I'd finally cracked the depression code! The next day, my mind pulled a bag over my head, whispered, "Playtime's over, bitch," and dragged me back "home." It's hard to conjure up the motivation to exercise every day, week, or month when you can't predict your mental state. And for those who suggest "pushing through the pain," here's a counteroffer: push an electric eel through your asshole.

Have you tried yoga?

I was doing yoga before I knew I was depressed. At my school, if you weren't on any of the sports teams, then you had to do yoga. I kept doing it after I realized I was depressed. I still do yoga now, and you're not going to believe this but I'M STILL SUPER DEPRESSED.

Have you tried taking vitamins?

Yes. Can they pull you out of suicidal ideation? No.

Have you tried crystals?

If by "try" you mean have I put crystals on my body to heal my chakras or whatever? Yes. Do I sound healed to you?

Have you tried acupuncture?

A week after I had acupuncture, I tried to kill myself. So there's that.

Have you tried living, laughing, loving?

I've tried one of those things and it was painful.

Have you tried looking in the mirror and saying, "I'M NOT CRAZY"?

Yes, and while it doesn't help my depression, it's very fun.

Have you tried breathing?

No, is it good?

Have you tried making a blood sacrifice to the gods of serotonin?

Yes, but I'm running out of blood.

Have you tried pretending to be happy?

Every. Day.

If you don't see one of your suggestions on the list, then I give you permission to climb a hill and shout your suggestion into the sky. If a person asks you for your opinion on their mental illness, then by all means give it to 'em. But if they don't, remember how free and relatively easy it is to keep your mouth shut. And if you're offended by anything in this chapter—if you feel hurt because I called you out on your curist ways—then in the legendary words of Tiffany "New York" Pollard, "You should've just sat there and ate your food."

Medication Vacations

I talk a big game when it comes to medication. I'm all, "Medication works," and "Medication saved my life," which is true. But, until now, there's a part of my medication story I've left out—the part where I stopped taking them. I'm not proud of it, but over the past few years I've taken myself off my meds for a variety of different, not to mention insane, reasons.

I'd been on a steady diet of medication for over a year before I convinced myself they weren't working. For the record, they were working for Amanda the person but not for Amanda the (I'm screaming and cringing while writing this). . . creative. That's right, I'd fallen into the classic trap of thinking that medication dulls your "creative genius." I'd been feeling stable for a couple of months; the depression, previously at a boiling point, was now at a low simmer. I was feeling, dare I say it, ok, and "ok" comes at a price. In the process of gaining control, must I lose my (cringing so hard right now) ability to create?

How could I be a writer without edge and scathing wit and all the other things I pretend to have?

It felt as though the meds had removed not only the imbalance in my brain but also an inherent piece of my personality. I'd lived with depression for so long that it felt like a natural part of me, like a bone or an ineptitude for basic math. It wasn't just depression; all aspects of my mental illness felt like home. The darkness inside me blossomed into a dangerous safe space—a place I could escape to when things got bad, somewhere I could go to feel worse, which in turn made me feel better. Throughout my childhood, I felt less than, and in my mind, I deserved to feel that way. I cannot speak for all Asian women, but in general, we grow up with a sense that we are not and never will be, good enough. No matter what we do, how hard we work, it will never be enough. We will never be enough. It's trauma like this that warps how we experience happiness.

I was left with an inability to process joy in a healthy way. And as a result, I am unable to digest good news like a normal human. For example, when my agent told me I had an offer on this book, I spiraled into suicidal ideation. Fucked up, right? But when you've grown up believing you're not good enough, and then someone says you might be, your traumatized brain has no idea what to do with this information. It's confusing. So you self-sabotage to get yourself back to "normal." The spiral downward made me feel better. I'd conflated light with darkness, and darkness with myself. And the fact that it got me this far meant that it should be credited, not pushed away.

So when the meds started to make me feel less horrendous, I didn't know how to handle it. My dangerous safe space wasn't as readily available as it had been in the past. It was the only "comfort" I'd known—like a freezing cold hug, but a hug nonetheless.

Even after a year of therapy, I was still convinced that my mental illness made me *me*. It's what got me a job, friends, people to have sex with, and most important, it's what *made* my writing. I was being gaslit by my mental illness, because in my mind I was nothing without it.

I stopped taking medication so I could get the "real" me back— the funny me, the creative me, the writer me. I didn't go cold turkey (because that would be crazy!). No no, in my super unprofessional opinion, I thought it best to "taper off," which just meant cutting my meds in half.

The first week of my totally cool and not at all dangerous experiment worked. I felt more alert and connected to others. The "real" me began to slither into my veins. Soon I would transform back into my all powerful, all fiery, all creative self! Things were going so well that I decided to take myself off meds completely! Mental illness, mental shmillness! I had cured myself! Like Jesus!

Three weeks in, my great plan started to unravel. The initial liveliness (in retrospect, restlessness) from week one had frittered away, and a deep depression took its place. But it was fine, I was fine, everything was FINE. In my inexpert medical opinion, it was natural to feel this way. Things had to get worse before they got better. Being depressed means it's working!

After a month, I was fully immersed in depression, and the suicidal thoughts resumed. By this time, I'd accepted that the plan had failed. I'd accepted that going off meds did not work. But none of that mattered, because I did *not* accept my mental illness. I was lost. I wasn't myself with meds, I wasn't myself without meds, and I was tired of fighting for myself. I know this sounds like an existential crisis (and maybe that was a part of it), but it was less "Who am I?" and more "I don't want to be whoever I am."

This all took place at the end of June 2014. By July 3, I was back in the hospital after my second suicide attempt.

I'm not saying medication is the key to psychiatric recovery, but taking myself off medication played a crucial part in my relapse. Unpacking a lifetime of depression and trauma in a little over a year combined with the medication version of Mr. Toad's Wild Ride proved a little too potent for my mental resolve.

Looking back, I realize that the meds were not keeping me from my "real" self; they were saving me from it. My "real" self was a fictional character I'd concocted to distract me from my mental illness. I often used it as a scapegoat—when everything got to be too much, I could say, "Well, at least this isn't me!"

The point is, meds kept me grounded and focused. They didn't dampen my creativity, and they didn't heighten it either. They made it possible for me to be creative without hurting. Has it changed how I write and approach writing? Yes. But for the better? Also yes. It's been said a thousand times before, but I'll say it again: Your creativity, humor, and work are not dictated by your mental illness. It does not give you an "edge," and honestly, if you're someone who *wants* an edge, then that's a whole other issue. ANYWAY, I learned my lesson, and I vowed to myself that I would never buy into the "meds make you less [fill in the blank]" myth again. But because I'm an absolute mess, even that difficult lesson didn't stop me from going off my meds for other reasons. Here are some other reasons I've stopped taking medication:

- Convinced myself I was not bipolar and that I'd been making this whole thing up.
- Wanted to induce hypomania so I could write faster (see the chapter titled "The Manic Mirage" for more details).
- Fell into a depressive episode and wanted to push myself over the edge.
- Was fed up with the routine.

I KNOW! I'm just as exhausted with myself as you are right now. And I'd love to say I can't help it, but I can. I want to be that person with the tidy pill holder and the can-do attitude, and I truly believe that one day I will buy a pill holder. The fact is, I'm still learning. There is no guidebook for this shit, which is good, because I wouldn't read it anyway. But if there is one rule we should all stick to, it would be take your meds . . . and talk to your therapist. Two rules—take meds and speak to therapist . . . and drink water. Ok, three rules. I'm going to stop now.

As always, do what works for you. And if you feel like going off your meds, try (if you can) to consult a doctor or psychiatrist first. Every time I've gone off my meds, I've done it alone. I didn't tell my therapist or my husband. The isolation and the lack of control compounded my depression. I became angry and defensive when my therapist inquired about my medication. I felt so ashamed for lying, and yet at the same time I believed it was for the best. When I did come clean with my therapist, I thought she'd be livid. I mean, I would be. If my patient told me they'd decided they could suddenly do my job with no formal training and took themselves off medication, I'd be like, "You fucking dickhead." And that is why I am not a therapist. But she wasn't mad at all; she was worried, and relieved I'd told her. I realized that in making my meds the enemy, I'd also turned on my therapist, my husband, and my entire support system. Taking meds is more than just realigning chemicals; it's a load-bearing Jenga piece in the tower of your mind. Remove it, and some shit is bound to fall.

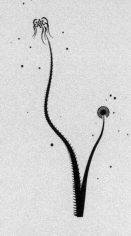

PART 4
Denial

All-Natural Depression
Face Masks

People often think depression looks a certain way: crying, sad, or just finished crying. But it's oh so much more than that! Depression is full of devastating layers. It runs deep and steady. I have an undercurrent of depression running through me at all times. Sometimes it's more pronounced; other times it's more Crouching Depression, Hidden Depression. But it's always there.

I'm still shocked that depressed people get told, "But you don't *look* depressed." Because, honestly, how goddamn dare you. Who are you to say whether somebody looks depressed or not? Please acquaint yourself with the life-changing magic of shutting the fuck up. The only person who's qualified to tell me whether I look depressed or not is my therapist and the guy who puts out the rotisserie chicken at my local Safeway.

The idea that something so deeply rooted in a person's mind would be identifiable via their face is absurd. You can't recognize depression in someone just by looking at them, because guess what? We look JUST. LIKE. YOU. Mwahahahaha! Isn't that terrifying, nondepressed people? It's impossible to tell who's depressed and who's not. We apply different facial expressions out of habit, not because we feel, but because we want to *appear* as though we do.

We wear these face masks for a multitude of reasons, includingto gain acceptance, to shield ourselves from shame, or to achieve an even, healthy glow.

Personally, I make a concerted effort to not look depressed in public, for the same reason I put on makeup – to lie to myself and others.

For those of you still unconvinced, allow me to present some of my lesser-known All-Natural Depression Face Masks.

Extremely Happy

An absolute staple. I have been donning Extremely Happy for years. Even though it's torturous to wear, it will make you feel like part of society even though you're dying inside. And isn't that what's truly important? Societal acceptance! Extremely Happy—it's the LBD (little black depression) for your face.

On-Point Professional

Who says you can't be depressed *and* good at your job? Probably most employers! On-Point Professional can be worn by anyone who works for a living. Inspire your coworkers with a face that says, "I get shit done!" even while you're mind says, "My mental condition is deteriorating, and I can't make it stop!" For those of you who work from home, don't worry! You can wear On-Point Professional on those rare occasions when you leave the house for a coffee or something and you want to make sure strangers on the street know you have a job because it's very important to impress people you don't (and will never) know. Very important.

Sheer Boredom

Boredom? How can you be bored when you have all this depression to be getting on with? What's my secret? I'll tell you: it's a two-in-one look! That's right, Sheer Boredom blends seamlessly with your depression. Think depression can be worn only with Crying? Think again! Sheer Boredom is one of the most popular depression looks to date. So what are you waiting for? Death? Me too!

Court Jester

I love this look because it's long-lasting and helps protect the wearer from any real feelings. Unlike Extremely Happy, Court Jester is so easy to wear that you'll forget you're wearing it! That is until you're alone and you have to take it off. Then it will hit you, hard. All those thoughts and feelings you thought you'd shielded yourself from by doing fun bits at parties? They're here now. It's just you and them and silence . . . until the next social event or after-work drinks or dinner party. Put Court Jester back on and let the laughter feed you! Haha! Who's laughing now? Not you!

Iridescent Indifference

Without a doubt, the coolest look of the bunch. Iridescent Indifference's unique numbing agent makes you look like an aloof French new wave film star on the outside while you continue to feel dead on the inside. You look at other people and wonder how and why they can be into *any activity*. You convince yourself that you're too cool for that shit, which maybe works for a while. Then you realize at least those people have shit they care about. You don't even have shit you *don't* care about. But at least you have Iridescent Indifference! Cool on the outside, nothing on the inside.

There you have it, just a few of my classic looks. If these don't resonate with you, then dig around inside yourself and see what you find. Or don't, because it's horrifying!

Lights, Camera, Depression

TV depression looks awesome. I'd love to have that kind of depression. And it's not just TV or depression; any mental illness on-screen looks pretty fucking cool. Either it's dark and dramatic—unlike day-to-day depression, which is at best super dull—or it's quirky and fleeting, like a flash sale of Zooey Deschanel's wardrobe.

Now, before you send me angry "actually" emails, I know there are shows out there that "get mental illness right," and yes, I have seen them. *Crazy Ex-Girlfriend*, *BoJack Horseman*, and *Lady Dynamite* are a few of the exceptions. I'm going to talk about the rules.

I grew up in a land before time (the nineties), a time when mental illness wasn't shown on TV at all. It was the golden age of teenage angst (*Dawson's Creek*, *My So-Called Life*, *Daria*), but diagnosed mental illness was never part of the story line. Back then, the big three were sex, alcohol, and drugs. Shows loved to weave a "dangers of drugs" narrative into special episodes. It's a wonder any of us managed to do recreational drugs after the infamous *Saved by the Bell* episode where Jessie gets addicted to "caffeine pills," although us cool kids knew it was speed (I did not know it was speed until just now). If you haven't seen the episode, all you need to know is that Jessie (Elizabeth Berkely) gets hooked on caffeine pills and ends up having a full meltdown in front of heartthrob Zach Morris (Half Asian Mark-Paul Gosselaar) while screaming, "I'm so excited!" It's a milestone in nineties cinematic history, so I suggest you look it up.

Teenage programming back then was so focused on sex, alcohol, and drug use that the shows often failed to include the psychology and motivations behind the sex, alcohol, and drug use. These topics were typically dealt with on a case-by-case basis rather than doing a deep dive into why someone would choose to abuse drugs or alcohol. And you know something? I didn't give a fuck. All I cared about was Pacey Witter and Joey Potter growing old together and adopting me as their fast-talking, pseudointellectual daughter, Amanda Witter-Potter.

During my formative years, the only time I saw mental illness represented was on the big screen—Hollywood, baby! I grew up watching movies in which beautiful, emaciated women went "full psycho" while their male counterparts went "crazy genius." If a woman was mentally ill she was an emotional wreck, throwing fits and hot crying. The men didn't have a mental illness so much as a "debonair madness," which only added to their appeal.

Angelina Jolie in *Girl, Interrupted*. Gena Rowlands in *A Woman Under the Influence*. Helena Bonham Carter in most of her films. Jack Nicholson in *One Flew Over the Cuckoo's Nest*. Brad Pitt in *Fight Club*. Russell Crowe in *A Beautiful Mind*. I remember watching these movies and thinking, "Mental illness is badass!" Not *real* mental illness, of course. Real mental illness was gross, and not cool at all. Silver screen mental illness was chic, risky, and worrisomely sexual.

Things have changed since then—not so much in movies, but in TV. We're seeing more mental illness on-screen than ever before.

Is that a good thing? Yes! And no! Broadly speaking, anytime we talk about mental health it is a good thing, but that doesn't mean spouting off any old shit (with the exception of this book). We still have to be responsible. Script words matter. As mentioned, there are a few shows today that "get" mental illness, but there are a whole bunch that don't. To that end, here are a few patterns I've noticed in the portrayal of mental illness on TV.

Diagnosis Never

Rarely do we hear an actual diagnosis in TV shows. We mostly have to guess that a character has either depression or anxiety, because that's pretty much all they show. Depression and anxiety seem to be the go-to mental illnesses for TV, as they're the easiest to manage and write. Unlike real life, TV characters can easily dip into and out of depression and anxiety. It's a convenient device for when a character gets a little dull, because you know what would spice up this scene? A panic attack. You know what would give this character "added depth"? A depressive episode. It's a nice little quirk to throw in, an easy way to up the stakes, and even easier to move on from. It's not like schizophrenia or bipolar—those ones you have to maintain the who-o-o-ole time, which can get so-o-o-o tedious. But there are some shows that buck that trend. Remember how Lena Dunham's character in *Girls* suddenly "got" OCD for like two episodes and then it was never mentioned again? That was fun. What I wouldn't give to have bipolar for just one season!

Edginess

Characters with mental illness are edgy as hell—like, what is their deal? They're often mysterious, or troubled, or mysteriously troubling. There are two types of edgy TV character: (1) has a dark aura about them and dresses as such, and (2) is kooky and "unique" in a Willy Wonka-esque way. There's no such thing as a humdrum mentally ill character; no one wants to see someone sleep till noon, get up, eat tuna from a can, and go back to sleep. It's a well-known fact that depression doesn't have one "look," but on TV it has two, and both are unrealistic.

One-Dimensionality

Some shows pick and choose when and for how long they want to show depression and anxiety. But for the shows that do commit to a character having a mental illness, that kinda becomes their "thing." They don't need much more depth if they have some sort of disorder. We talk about how your mental illness doesn't define who you are, but on TV you *are* your mental illness. People will ask, "Who's that actor on that show? Y'know, the one who plays the schizo?" or "She's on that teen show, the suicide one," and of course, "She's the one who goes insane." I know, aside from a quick internet search, this may be the fastest way to find out an actor's name, but it just goes to show how one-dimensional some of these characters can be.

The Cause of All Bad Things

Characters make bad choices all the time; it's what creates great television. Whenever someone takes a wrong turn, it drives the plot forward and further immerses us in the story. But it's not just TV. It's human nature to fuck up, and that's sometimes what makes life kind of thrilling too. Whether you have a mental illness or not, we all make bad decisions. Most of my bad decisions have come from me being a terrible person and have nothing to do with my bipolar. However, in TV land, characters are almost always driven to the brink by their mental illness. Whether it's murder, burning down a building, or causing a scene at a society party, it's the "crazy" that's to blame. If it weren't for that pesky personality disorder, they'd be all good! I'm not saying characters with a mental illness should be portrayed as angels, far from it! But if they're shitbags, make them shitbags for the right reasons—because deep down, they're shitbags.

Malevolent Meds

There's no scarier villain than medication! When has anyone ever taken medication regularly on TV with minimal drama? Meds are a perfect plot device because they are built to cause trouble. If you don't take them? Trouble. If you take too many? Trouble. If they're the wrong type of meds? Trouble. There are so many exciting combinations and outcomes of how meds can mess you up, but there's nothing titillating about someone routinely taking their medication and "doing fine." A lot of the problematic opinions I had about meds were formed by how they were depicted on TV. It seemed like all they ever did was cause mayhem and heartbreak for the people who needed them.

High Drama

I'm always surprised by how dramatic mental illness is on-screen. I've never known depression to be so jam-packed, but on TV it seems so exhausting. In my TV show, there'd be about three nap breaks before Act Two. How do these characters have the energy to be so demonstrably depressed all the time? I mean, sure, I'm depressed all the time, but I can't be visibly tortured and crying every hour. I still have to, like, go to the bank! A realistic depressed character is a repressed one. It's not all outbursts and meltdowns; it's mostly just "trying to get by" and "trying to get out of stuff." I understand that TV shows have to be entertaining, and I enjoy watching characters have meltdowns as much as the next person. My only wish is to see more than one side of mental illness. By all means, give us the hysteria and catastrophes, but balance it out with the drab and insipid.

White Wail

Diversity in representation has always been a mess in Hollywood, but damn, I didn't know only white people could be mentally ill! Don't get me wrong, white people are crazy for sure, but when they're the only ones we *see* struggling with mental health issues, it makes it seem like they're the only ones who are *allowed* to have mental health issues. It contributes to an "it could never happen to me" attitude.

I never saw anyone who looked like me deal with mental health issues in any form of media, so I assumed it never happened to Asian people. I rarely saw other Asian people in movies, but when I did the characters were either serious, sensible, stoic, or all three. The closest I ever got to seeing myself in a movie was in *The Joy Luck Club*. Even though I was seven when that movie came out, I could relate to the younger women purely because they'd grown up in Western society and weren't the stereotypical stoic Chinese daughters. I connected to the intense and strained relationships they had with their mothers. I wasn't stoic or reserved, I was emotional and liked hugging. I didn't want the silent treatment, I wanted to talk it out. How can I know what I've done wrong if no-one will talk to me? I sought advice from my older cousin, who's more like an older sister. She'd been on the receiving end of the stony silence many times before me, but all she could do was shrug and say, "that's how it is in our family, you know that." I felt like ours was the only family who operated in this way, and I felt like the only half-Chinese girl who didn't fit into her full-Chinese family. *The Joy Luck Club* was the first time I realized it wasn't just my family and it wasn't just me. To this day, I can't get through it without bawling my fucking eyes out, not just because it's a great movie, but because all those years ago, it was the hug I so desperately needed.

The next time I'd see a movie where the entire cast was Asian-American and British East Asian (and not doing martial arts) would be twenty five years later with *Crazy Rich Asians*. I don't need to tell you that when Eleanor Young (played by Her Royal Highness, Michelle Yeoh) tells Constance Wu's Rachel Chu that she will "never be enough" I had a goddamn aneurysm. And I have no shame in telling you that I'm crying while writing this, because THIS IS THE EFFECT REPRESENTATION HAS.

Of course, it's not just Asians. There are millions of people who rarely see themselves in mainstream movies, let alone see themselves living with mental illness —people of color, LGBTQ+ folks, and people with disabilities.

Mental illness does not discriminate, it does not look a certain way, and it's more common than the common cold. It's not just straight, white, ethereal-looking people who get depression. Asian people are depressed. Black people are depressed. Queer people are depressed. Trans people are depressed. People with disabilities are depressed. WE'RE ALL DEPRESSED! Let us in on the depression action!

This is my plea to Hollywood or anyone thinking of making a show or movie that includes mental illness: First, I know I may sound like an utter killjoy, so please understand that I love the drama and hyperbole of television and film. I don't want to remove the "entertainment factor" from any show depicting mental illness. But I do think it's important to present a balanced view. Show us the soul-crushing downs *and* the mundane ups. We want to see mental illness in all its terrible glory, from every angle and every background. If you want your character to be "dark and edgy," then go for it—but make sure there's more to them than their illness, because that's how it works in real life with us mere mortals. Think twice before you make someone "dangerous" or "threatening" purely because of their mental disorder or use of medication. Just be responsible. As filmmakers, you have an immense influence on mental illness and its stigma. And I would know, because for the first eighteen years of my life, everything I knew about mental illness I learned from you.

You Can Be Either Mentally Ill or an Asshole or Both

Just because I have a mental illness doesn't mean I'm incapable of being a dick. And while there are a few aspects of life where being mentally ill holds me back, being a jerk is not one of them.

Ok, now this sounds like I'm a horrible person. I'm not. I'm a good friend. I'll support you through breakups, life changes, and day-to-day shittiness. I will immediately hate anyone you hate, no questions asked. When you ask me to take a photo of you, I will take *at least* eleven, from different yet flattering angles. I won't pick you up from the airport, but then again I'll never ask you to pick me up from the airport either. Good friend indeed, although not too good to be true. Here are some examples.

I've held grudges longer than *Law and Order* has been on the air, and I'll continue to do so well into the afterlife (when *Law and Order* will still be on the air). These grudges are aided and abetted by a stubbornness usually reserved for a teenage bull with an early curfew. The phrase "cut off your nose to spite your face" never made sense to me. Why stop at just the nose? I'd Cage/Travolta my face to spite my entire body. My pettiness knows no bounds. I once joked to a friend that if she died before me, I'd kill myself at her funeral to pull focus. It was A JOKE, also she said she wouldn't be surprised. Anyway, I'm straying into horrible-person waters, so let me get back on land.

The point is my shortcomings have nothing to do with my mental illness. When I snap at you because I've had to repeat myself more than once, it's not because I'm depressed; it's because I hate repeating myself. (Side note: an ex once told me that this refusal to repeat oneself was very "self-important," and from that moment I vowed never to repeat myself again—as I said, boundless petti-ness.) If I get unreasonably angry because you're late for a movie date, it's not because I'm manic; it's because I love trailers. Trailers are the windows to movies' souls, and if you deprive me of that, you deserve my ire.

Similarly, if you get annoyed with *me* for any number of reasons and *I* become upset, do not think for one minute it's because I have a mental illness; it's because I'm a baby woman who's terrified of confrontation.

People sometimes assume that a person is behaving a certain way because of their illness when they're just being their usual, "normal" selves. These assumptions are at best annoying and at worst dangerous.

Good friends usually know when you're being yourself. They tend not to lead with "Oh, that must be the bipolar." In fact, when I'm going through a depressive episode, I don't typically go out or see my friends, so there's nothing to judge. Those close to me know when I'm "going through it" because I either (a) drop off the map completely, (b) text the group chat informing them I'm ok but going through some shit, or (c) tweet incessantly about it.

Friends and acquaintances outside the core group (core group = five people because I'm over the age of twenty-eight) may think differently, and I don't blame them. I used to make the same assumptions about people with depression. Why is this person not laughing at my joke? Must be the depression. Why does this person need to go to the bathroom? I guess it's the depression. Why is this person breathing? Depression, of course! It was only later that I realized people who have depression rarely behave depressed in public. Instead, we act like we're fine and everything's fine and wow look at how fine this all is! For the most part, I save my crazy for private home time, which is all well and good as long as you don't live with someone. I live with someone. I live with someone I have sex with and to whom I am married. I know I said people close to you understand when you're being yourself, but it's a whole different ball game when it's someone you live with and who knows you inside out. The thing about my high-functioning depression is that the high-functioning part can remain in place during the day, but come nightfall the facade crumbles and I transform back, much like a werewolf but with more trauma. It's tough hiding temperamental behavior from your partner because, like, they're always around. When you live with someone, nothing is sacred. Your crying closet is not *your* closet anymore; now someone else's pants are in here, ugh. You can't lie on the floor and howl awkwardly in peace because chances are someone will interrupt to ask if you're ok, at which point you have to stop and gesture at your entire self. There are times when you want to sit quietly and stare into nothingness and think about every bad thing that's ever happened to you because you really want to lean into the sadness. Of course, all the things I mentioned are not exclusive to mental illness, but they're also not *not* exclusive to it either. You can see how tricky it would be for a live-in loved one to decipher whether you're depressed or just sad misc. And this kind of confusion can put a lot of strain on a relationship.

Over the years, I've had countless arguments with my partner (as every good couple should). We've argued about everything from "I don't care if you want to go out, just let me know first so I can make my own plans" to "Would it kill you to hang your towel up?" to "Get out of my apartment." We also argue about big, adult stuff like money, finances, and money. Whatever we argue about—whether it's big or "socks go *in* the laundry basket"—my partner has, more than once, inferred that it has stemmed from my mental disorder. He'd stop me midargument and ask, "Did you take your meds today?" Not in a jokey way—in a serious way, which somehow hurts more. Aside from the implication that I'm acting this way only because I'm not suppressed by medication, it's the presumption that I can't be arguing with you in a *real* way, with *real* emotions, and that what I'm experiencing is not real. That's what stings. It's the idea that I'm not the correct person who should be having this argument. It feels as though I'm the Hulk and someone's shouting, "IS BRUCE BANNER IN THERE? WE'D LIKE TO SPEAK TO BRUCE, PLEASE."

Asking if I've taken my medication halfway through an argument immediately renders any next move useless, it's like a Catch-Twenty Fuck. If I say no, then it's like "point proven." If I say yes, then what? Then we carry on arguing because I've provided a satisfactory answer? By giving any response, I'm validating your invalidation of me. So, let me be clear, I'm not fighting with you about socks because I'm mentally ill; I'm fighting with you because I truly believe, deep in my soul, that socks belong in the fucking laundry basket. Same goes for being dramatic, attention-seeking, and lazy. I'm all those things, not because I'm ill; but because I'm a messy bitch who lives for drama. Yes, there's a difference.

There are many variations on "Have you taken your meds today?" There's "Have you spoken to your therapist today?" or

"Is this because you were depressed last week?" and of course "Maybe I should call someone?" Some of you might be thinking, "What awful and passive-aggressive things to say to someone with a mental illness," and you'd be right! To be fair to my partner, he doesn't say shit like this anymore. It took a lot of talking and "working through," but we're good now. We still argue though, OH WE ARGUE, just not about my mental health.

As much as it pains me to back down from anything ever, I do empathize with my partner. It's not easy living with someone who has a mental illness (but if you do, then you're not some hero, so settle down). Chances are you've seen a breakdown or two hundred in your time, and those can be terrifying for everyone involved. It makes sense that one may conflate regular ol' anger or sorrow with mania or depression. These assumptions and comments don't come from a place of malice but rather out of fear and worry. My partner isn't saying these things to hurt me; he's saying them to make sure I don't hurt myself. That's always been his biggest concern. And can you blame him? He watched me get hospitalized after I tried to kill myself (the second time). I'm ashamed to say that it took a while for me to appreciate the toll that takes on another person. I can't imagine what it must be like to see someone you love harm themselves. And I've done it several times. But at no point, even at my lowest lows, have I ever wanted to harm another person.

Those who know me know there is no way in hell I'd physically hurt them (emotionally maybe, but never physically). Even with my assholeness and mental illness combined, the only person I'd ever harm would be myself. And that goes for most people who have a mental illness. Mentalhealth.gov recently reported that only 3 to 5 percent of violent acts can be attributed to individuals living with a mental illness, and those with severe mental illness are ten times more likely to be victims of violence than the general population. When we look at the violent acts committed by this small group, we see that the violence often occurred during a high-risk period, either during a first-time psychotic episode or shortly after inpatient psychiatric hospitalization. This means that the violence committed by a mentally ill person is often out of the person's control.

My first psychotic episode felt like it came out of nowhere. In the days leading up to it, I felt "normal", maybe a little more stressed than usual, but nothing out of the ordinary. I went to work, I ate three meals a day, I watched *Parks and Recreation*—things most humans do. The one thing that felt eerily unfamiliar was my ability to repress my feelings, or rather, the lack thereof. For most of my life, swallowing darkness had become second nature, like breathing or making that "oop" sound when you bump into someone. Keeping it all down is what kept me safe. Any trauma, big or small, I would quash immediately without even thinking. My brother's death? Quashed. Bad breakup? Quashed. My capacity to quash? Quashed. But that reflex started to give out. And now every time someone said anything remotely hurtful, it didn't bounce off me like I was Teflon; it poured straight through me like molten lava. What the fuck was happening? Why was I . . . *feeling*?

My mind was so preoccupied with this new sensation that I could barely concentrate on anything else. I wasn't acting like a douche, nor was I acting like a fragile flower, I was just . . . acting. I'd reverted back to my natural state, a state familiar to those with a mental illness: survival mode. And it's *this* behavior that is most heavily influenced by my mental illness, not being an asshole or being sensitive or being overly dramatic. Those are all *me*. It's when I'm *not* those things that you should start to question my mental state. You shouldn't be worried when I get angry, annoyed, or butthurt. You should be worried when I'm *happy*.

The breakdown was hurtling toward me at full speed. And although I felt my mind slipping away, I did everything I could to hide it—not just from other people, but also from myself.

This was one of the lowest point in my life, a few days before my first suicide attempt, but there was no part of me that wanted to physically harm another person.

Most of the time, mental illness is seen as a burden and an unnecessary government expense—until a racist, white, American male commits a violent crime. That's when mental illness gets trotted out like a show pony at a state fair. Meanwhile, those of us who have a mental illness are forced to sit and watch this play out. Every single time. Whether it's politicians pretending to care about mental health, the media perpetuating the myth that mentally ill people are dangerous, or even a partner asking if you're sure you took your meds, it's exhausting. When I see debates on the news regarding violence and mental illness, it feels almost surreal. They're talking about someone like me, but also about someone who's nothing like me. Most of the time it doesn't feel like they're talking about *people*. No wonder folks are scared of us! We sound like goddamn killing machines! It's a false flag. Most mentally ill people I know can barely get out of bed before noon, let alone go out and attack someone. And during the times when I do have mental illness–induced energy—a.k.a. hypomania—I can barely focus, like a coked-up magpie at Tiffany's.

It's hard enough living with mental illness without the patrolling eyes of the government, the media, and, sometimes, your own peers. In addition to feeling depressed, anxious, and suicidal, we must also take the time to assure people that we don't want to harm them. It's a lose-lose situation. The people who are scared of our "violent tendencies" are often the same people who call suicide a selfish act that could have been prevented. Damned if you do, and dead if you don't!

We're not perfect by any means, but people with mental illness aren't the monsters some make us out to be. We're just like you, and it's possible for us to be dicks without any ulterior mentalness. Not only is it possible, it's natural. Just like the rest of the human race, it's our god-given right to be awful!

Mental illness is complex and ever changing. It's specific to the individual; there's no "one size fits all." My depression is different from your depression is different from your friend's depression. And while each of us experiences the illness in our own way, the majority of us are harmless.

When it comes to assholery, there are times when we need to ghost friends or cancel last minute. We need to do it for our own sanity, and I'll get to that later. What's not ok is when we're purposely unkind or disrespectful and blame it on our mental illness. When we use our illness as a scapegoat, we contribute to the stigma. I know. Look at me sounding like an inspirational mental health influencer. But as you know, I'm not any of those things, because yes, I have used my mental illness as a shield many times. I'm still trying to walk the walk.

Mental illness doesn't define who you are. It also doesn't define your shitty behavior. And I'm doing my best to hold myself accountable for my actions so that other people won't do it for me. So, when it comes to my character, leave my illness out of it. Don't judge me based on my mental illness; judge me for the asshole I am.

Excuses, Excuses, Excuses

When you have a mental illness, the cover-up is real. Almost every day, you're faced with a slew (if you're popular) of invites to social events or (if you're me) general life admin that requires leaving the house and talking to strangers. Whatever it is, anything outside of staying indoors can drain you of the little mental energy you have left. And when you're at an especially low point, even something as benign as moving from the couch to the bed can feel like wading through quicksand. Reticence to go out to a club, bar, or party isn't exclusive to those with mental illnesses. There are countless memes and tweets about being an "introvert" and "creaming yourself when someone cancels on you." I love depression memes. They're eye-wateringly accurate and make me feel less alone. But once you're offline, you're alone, and that friend's get-together you just tweeted about, is tonight.

Having a mental illness doesn't mean you don't like to be sociable or don't have the ability. I joke a lot about how I hate people, but only 60 percent of that is true. I like connecting with friends; it's one of the few things that helps me stay sane. If I'm being honest, there are loads of events, parties, and milestones I'd love to attend. Sometimes I'm a lazy piece of shit and won't go, but there are times when going feels impossible. There's a difference between "I can't be bothered" and "I physically and mentally can't do this." People understand the difference in *theory*, but they're often unwilling to accept it in practice.

Once my depression started to flourish, halfway through college, I stopped going out. I was thenceforth known as a *flake*. I'd been given the reputation of someone who was unreliable and generally uninterested. People would say, "You could invite Amanda, but I guarantee she won't come." On the odd occasion when I did make an appearance, I'd be mocked with, "Well look who decided to grace us with her presence!" People assumed I didn't care, and I let them. I let them think I was this apathetic flake who hated Good Times, because the reality was much worse. I couldn't bring myself to say, "I can't come out. I'm struggling with my mental health. I think I might be depressed but I'm not sure. I don't know what to do. Please help." I can barely say that now! Just thinking about it gives me (additional) anxiety. It's a real testament to the mental illness stigma when you'd rather let your friends think you're a shitty person than tell them the truth about how you feel.

I leaned into the flake persona, which made maintaining friendships hard but coming up with excuses super easy. After a while I didn't even need excuses, because people just stopped inviting me to shit. On the rare occasions an invitation was extended, I continued to isolate myself not by making up a reason why I couldn't attend but by refusing to *give* a reason. I was ashamed, and I was worried about how people would react. I didn't want them to think I was weird and stop hanging out with me. Instead, they thought I was indifferent and stopped hanging out with me. Word of wisdom: weird beats indifferent every time.

Making excuses for your mental illness is all part of the tragic package. It starts with a few white lies here and there: "I can't come out, I have a bad headache," or "My pet is sick," or "Oh my god, was that tonight?" Harmless. But you can't keep using the same three excuses, just like you can't wear the same outfit three days in a row—or so I've been told, repeatedly. So you craft new excuses, and workshop them like a tight five. They become more intricate; some require a backstory. And before you know it you have a mental Rolodex full of excuses, enough to fill the grandest of canyons.

These excuses become your lifeline. You tend to them and care for them like you would plants or a strong personal brand. After a while they become second nature and start rolling off your tongue:

"You coming tonight?"

"I wish! I have dinner with my cousin who literally just flew in last night and didn't tell anyone other than me because she's currently going through some shit with my aunt. Ugh, it's a whole thing, but I promised I'd see her. Have fun though!"

I wrote that excuse in one go. Didn't need to think. It's like breathing.

There comes a point when you have an excuse for every occasion, because it's not just parties and evening activities that require mental fortitude. It's A N Y T H I N G.

- Coffee catch-ups
- Housewarmings
- Baby showers
- A "quick bite somewhere"
- A business lunch
- Any meeting
- BBQs
- "We're watching it at ours, you should come"
- Any party connected to a wedding—engagement, bachelorette, shower, brunch

- Group shopping trips (and by *group* I mean shopping with anyone other than myself)
- Anything described as a "little get-together" or "small gathering of folks"
- Hikes

To the non–mentally ill eye, these may seem like normal, enjoyable activities, but when you have depression, anxiety, or most other mental disorders, they look like obstacle courses located deep within the devil's butthole. Don't get me wrong—I wouldn't mind going to a BBQ or even a housewarming, but it's a little difficult to feign interest in your bathroom's subway tiles while trying to hide my panic sweats. It doesn't mean I never go out or never respect adult obligations; I've been to plenty of coffees, quick bites, and parties that I've hated. But I didn't go because I wanted to; I went because I wasn't depressed that day. If I can go, I will.

It takes a lot to tell your friends you "can't make it" for the millionth time. The guilt eats away at you, and you beat yourself up for being so feeble. You blame yourself for something you can't control. And even though you're glad you've decided to stay in and look after yourself, you somehow feel worse. But I'm going to let you in on a secret: YOU ARE NOT TO BLAME. There, all better now.

Seriously, though, if you are going through some shit and cannot handle mass social interaction, then do what you need to do. If that means staying indoors and binge-watching *Brooklyn Nine-Nine* (highly recommended and possibly doctor prescribed), then do it. You shouldn't feel bad about looking after yourself, and other people shouldn't make you feel bad for looking after yourself. Sure, it'd be ideal if all conversations could go like this:

Friend: "You coming out tonight?"

You: "Can't tonight. Having a rough time with my mental health at the moment."

Friend: "Sorry to hear that. Do you need anything? Want me to come over?"

You: "Nah, I'm good. Thank you though. Have fun!"

Friend: "Alright, cool. I'll drop you a text tomorrow or something."

You: "Cool."

Maybe some of you have these conversations, which is wonderful, the more open and non-judgmental conversations, the better! But for a lot of people, these interactions are a human centipede of stigma: We can't tell our friends the truth > because we're scared and/or uncomfortable > because Society > so people will never know the truth > so they won't be able to help > and they'll assume we're just being dicks > because Society > . . . and so on.

We'd all love to live in a world where we can be honest about our mental illness, where telling someone, in person, that we're grappling with our mental health is commonplace. And even though awareness has improved, especially since I was diagnosed, there's still more work to do. We want to be at a point where talking about mental illness becomes not only natural, but ideally, mundane. One day, but until then here are some of my not-ideal-but-what-else-you-got solutions:

For those with a mental illness

- ONLY if you feel up to it, be honest about why you don't want to go out. We won't know how people will react if we don't try. If they react badly, fuck 'em. I'm sure there's a more mature way to manage that outcome, but, honestly, I'm too old and tired.

- If you do end up telling someone the truth as to why you can't come out, and they seem uncomfortable or confused, that's ok. You don't need to explain yourself further. You've done your bit. Just understand that this may be new for them too, and it may take a while to process.

For everyone else

- If you have a friend who consistently comes up with excuses to not go out, do NOT label them a flake. Do NOT dismiss them. There may be something else going on (or maybe they just don't like you). If you are concerned at all, simply ask if they're ok. If they say, "Yeah," chances are they're not ok but they don't want to talk about it right now. In which case, just remind them that you're there for them and you hope to catch up soon.

- If you're at a bar or party, and your friend says they're leaving early, do NOT persuade them to stay. Do NOT say shit like "Don't be such a pussy!" or "Just stay for one more drink." Do NOT question them with "Why? All you're gonna do is go to bed," or "Why? We don't have work tomorrow." None of these things matter. If someone wants to go home, LET THEM GO HOME. You don't know what they're going through. Maybe they're feeling overwhelmed (or maybe they just don't like you). Either way, be cool. Let them go in peace, ask them to text you when they get home so you know they're safe, and drop them a check-in text the next day.

I understand how frustrating it must be to be on the receiving end of my excuses; it doesn't make for Good Times and can put a strain on friendships. I understand that you can't help me if I don't tell you what's wrong, but you need to understand that I don't want this either. All jokes aside, I do want to come to your party even though I know it'll be shit. Believe me, I want to see you and our friends, and if I can I will. But I need you to understand that sometimes I can't, and I need you to be ok with that.

I promise to be more honest with you if you promise to never invite me on a hike. Deal? Deal.

The Manic Mirage

I once had an overwhelming urge to draw. I don't draw. I'm not good at drawing, but I wanted to fucking DRAW. I drew pictures all day, every day for a week. Anything I could see, I drew: people, water bottles, bananas, real thought-provoking stuff. I filled two notebooks in a week and remember thinking to myself, "This is how Picasso must have felt."

There was another time when I didn't sleep for three days. I spent my nights applying for jobs I wasn't qualified for. Between sending in my resume for university professor and museum curator, I impulse-bought things I didn't need (aroma diffusers and every book Amazon recommends). If buying a ton of random stuff at 3:01 a.m. sounds normal to you, great, but it's not usually my thing. I'm—how can I put this?—really fucking cheap.

Earlier this year, I wrote ten thousand words in one day. I'm not a fast writer usually. Still, I continued to write and rewrite. After four days I had written a book, and not just any book—I'd written the greatest book of all time. Now, this may come as a shock, but I'm not Picasso. I never got that job as a lead animator at Pixar. And I'm not some prodigious writer. So how did I write the Great American Novel in less than a week? The answer is I didn't. I was in a manic state. When I came to, I looked back at my "work" and saw that it was a mess lacking in both quality and coherence. It was devastating. It was a humiliating fall from grace, like waking up after a one-night stand only to see that there was no one there to begin with.

As a mentally ill person, I constantly feel like a lazy, unproductive nonmember of society. But when I'm hypomanic, I'm *the* main contributor to society. I'm essential, like Oprah or memes, or Oprah memes.

For those who don't know, hypomania is a mild form of mania. Its symptoms include increased energy, confidence, and impulsivity. And it can make you extremely talkative. It sounds like a fucking nightmare, and I assure you it is. However, for someone who's depressed most of the time, hypomania is intoxicating. It makes you feel invincible, like you have the confidence of a white man who writes "I get shit done" in his LinkedIn bio, except you're *actually* doing shit. It's the best of both worlds. For one brief, shining moment, you feel useful—then it's gone, and you have nothing to show for it.

The aftermath of a manic episode is sobering. I don't know how it works with other people, but I fall into a deep depression, followed by a review of all the "work" I produced. Only when I look back at the fruits of my productivity do I realize I'm not Frida Kahlo reincarnate. I just drew a bunch of hand turkeys.

We've been conditioned to see mania as an awesome bonus that accompanies mental illness rather than a dangerous by-product. It's like watching a person with the flu froth at the mouth and thinking, "That'll help with decongesting." But there is nothing useful about mania. It doesn't make you productive or a creative genius; it just makes you *think* you are. And no matter how many sexy-insane characters Aubrey Plaza plays, there's nothing cool about it.

Hollywood would beg to disagree. To them, mental illness is prime Oscar bait. Producers love to make mania this dramatic, intriguing asset that's disguised as a flaw. They show us Carrie Mathison using mania to solve terrorism in *Homeland*, or Monica being a supermom in *Shameless*. But we don't often see the traumatic days that ensue—the overwhelming depression and debilitating exhaustion. That doesn't make for good TV, of course.

The angst-ridden teenage Amanda thought mental illness was super edgy and enigmatic. There was something refreshing about how artists like Ian Curtis and Kurt Cobain wore their pain on the outside. It made them seem authentic. At the time, I didn't understand that this "authenticity" was just a flattering filter applied to a very ugly disorder. I thought the "tortured artist" thing was very cool. I was seduced by the idea that depression and mania unlocked some sort of mystical creative power. With great art comes great mental illness!

Before I was diagnosed with bipolar II disorder, I 100 percent believed in this shit. To me, when it came to being creative, you didn't have to be crazy to make things, but it helped. How else could you create so much incredible work at such an alarming rate if you weren't tormented in some way?

At that point, I still didn't recognize my mania as a mental illness. My friends didn't recognize it either. They may have just seen me as "excitable." I saw this temporary whimsical state wherein your mind whisked you away for a few days to create beautiful music and poetry. It wasn't attached to a larger mental health issue, psychological trauma, depression, or psychosis. Mania was sweet. Mental illness was scary. The two were not the same, I thought—that is, until I experienced it myself.

I first started recognizing my manic episodes about five years ago, and the worst thing about them was how good they made me feel. When I was manic, I felt prolific and alive. I had spent so much of my life feeling depressed, pointless, and suicidal, but then, BOOM! Mania took over, and suddenly I wanted to LIVE and DO THINGS.

When I'm manic, I become obsessed with one goal. I don't eat or sleep, and I sweat a lot. I'm filled with an unhealthy amount of confidence. I suffer from terrifying delusions of grandeur. (Not like the ones I have in real life where I'm friends with Beyoncé—or the ones where I think I *am* Beyoncé, or at least the Beyoncé of the literary world, who I assume would also be Beyoncé.) I talk faster and louder than usual. I'm irritable and prone to flying into a rage at any moment. On the inside, I feel like Mozart in the movie *Amadeus* screaming at Salieri, "Do you have it? Do you have it?" On the outside, I'm barking nonsense at a succulent on my window sill.

Some may think it's like being on drugs, and they'd be right, but they're not fun drugs. It's like being on a cocktail of meth and jet fuel for five days straight. The comedown is horrific, and it takes about a week to get back to "normal." All you have to show for it are pages of gibberish and poor personal hygiene.

I'm embarrassed to admit that I have purposefully summoned my mania, similar to how Nancy invokes Manon in *The Craft*, only with fewer candles. It's irresponsible and stupid on so many levels. When I don't take my meds, I don't just experience mania; I go through a whole roller coaster of shit. It's not like my mind can just churn out one clean manic episode. So if I want that hypomania, I have to be willing to further damage my mental health.

Nowadays, I don't do it to tap into my "creative genius" (which is absolutely not a thing) but to create false feelings of productivity and usefulness. I know nothing will come of it, but when it comes to my mental illness, sometimes living a lie feels so much better than owning a truth.

My hypomania has never put me in dangerous situations. It's relatively mild compared to *mania* mania. It makes me more reckless with my finances, relationships, and personal hygiene. The real danger with a hypomanic episode is what comes after it's over: the depression, the feelings of hopelessness, and the suicidal ideation. It's the sense of foolishness from thinking you'd outsmarted your own mind, only to find it was just another trap. The manic episode itself feels like you're outrunning the Road Runner. The aftermath is like finding out there's nothing under your feet and you're holding an anvil.

Everyone experiences mania and hypomania differently, but I don't know anyone who's ever felt good after a manic episode. What I do know is that mania does not help you do your best work or be your best self. It doesn't even help you do *good* work or be your *good* self. I can safely say that all of my best work has come from a nonmanic state. My productivity and focus come from taking my medication, getting good sleep, and being fortunate enough to see a therapist.

These days I'm more depressed than manic, and this may sound strange, but I'm pleased with that. I'm content. There's no expectation with depression. You're already at your lowest ebb, but at least it's real. Mania, on the other hand, is just lies. The confidence, the grandeur, the productivity is all just an illusion—like a shell company in Panama, No More Tears shampoo, or literally anything on *The Bachelor*.

The tortured-artist persona is another lie. Take me, for example: I'm a writer who happens to have a mental illness, and I'm not sitting at an antique bureau surrounded by piles of manuscripts with a cigarette in one hand and a quill in the other. I'm in bed, crouched over my laptop like a freelance Gollum, eating Cheerios straight from the box. (I assume most writers write like this. If not, then I apologize. Please continue with your perfect life.)

Whether it's making mania look sexy or creative or threatening, when we glamorize these afflictions we belittle them. If we ignore the aftereffects or the day-to-day life of someone with a mental illness, we dilute the reality. All that's left is a slice of drama, and mental illness isn't just drama. It's scary, and tiring, and boring, and ugly, and normal—just like the rest of life. We're not extraordinary because we have a mental illness; we're extraordinary because we survive it every single day.

I still wrestle with my feelings toward mania. All I can do is continue to take care of myself as best I can. Mania may make me feel alive for a second, but if it's a choice between being a real, depressed Gollum or a fake, pompous Mozart, then you'll have to excuse me—I have a box of Cheerios to attend to.

PART 5

Relationships

"Hello, I'm Mental": Too Much?

We talk about talking about mental illness a lot, which is great, and important, and great. The more we talk about mental illness, the more we normalize it, which is great, and important, and great. But when I was starting out as a fledgling mental, I didn't know *how* to talk about it. The only people I'd talk to about my mental illness were my mother (not great), my doctors (good but doctor-y), and my fellow patients (good and mental like me). The only acceptance I gained came from within the mental health community, and although it was comforting to have that reassurance, I wasn't going to be surrounded by doctors and patient friends my whole life. I had to get back out there, return to work, and deal with *sharp intake of breath* other people.

After my second suicide attempt and subsequent stint in rehab, I vowed to be more vocal about my mental health—mainly because it was the one solution I hadn't tried and, also, I didn't want to end up back in rehab. Rehab was nothing like the psychiatric hospital in Boston. For starters, it was a luxury hotel turned rehabilitation center based in the Bay Area, which overlooked Richardson Bay—the farthest of cries from the gothic woodlands of Belmont, Massachusetts. Everything was very fancy. It felt a lot more like a country club (or what I assume a country club feels like, based on the movies) than rehab, but I believe that's what most rehabs feel like these days. I dunno. I'm not an expert. I'm sure rehab works for a lot of people, but this did not work for me at all, probably due to the fact that the center was focused more on alcohol and drug abuse than on psychiatric rehabilitation. But no one knew where else to put me. The staff were lovely and the facilities were great, but the whole atmosphere just seemed a little too . . . chill.

Back in Boston, we'd had a strict schedule. In the morning after breakfast, we'd meet individually with the head psychiatrist to discuss general well-being and medication. The rest of the day was filled with one-on-ones with different psychiatrists who each had a specific specialty. We'd have a group session in the late afternoon, and, if it was approved, we could go on a trip into town accompanied by a member of staff. This may seem like a lot of activity, but we had downtime between sessions, which I spent either drawing, reading, or doing puzzles. I loved the routine. I craved the routine. It made me feel grounded and in control, which is key when you feel like you've lost your entire mind. The routine gave me a sense of purpose; even the act of attending a session made me feel like I'd achieved something. Working through a psychotic break was rough, but having a schedule, along with constant support and careful monitoring, made it a whole lot easier.

Why didn't you go back to Boston then? I hear you cry. Great question. And to be perfectly honest, it's because I had a dog. The hospital in Boston didn't allow pets, but this local rehab did. I acquired a dog during a manic episode, thinking it would solve all my problems, and it did. If you're mentally ill, get a dog; they're the only cure. Benny (my miracle dog cure) was still a puppy at the time, which helped to instill a sense of responsibility, but it didn't help with the whole I-can't-look-after-myself-let-alone-another-living-creature situation.

Benny is a thirteen-pound shih tzu who looks exactly like an Ewok. He's the sweetest little pup. He's never bitten or even growled at a person or another dog. He rarely barks, but when he does it's only because he wants to play, which is also rare because Benny is lazy. When people come to visit, they often forget there's a dog in the house. They say, "he's more like a cat," and I don't know how to take that.

So here I was, fresh off another suicide attempt, on my way, with my dog, to a waterfront rehab center for substance abuse. To complicate things further, because I don't like to half-ass making life harder for myself, I'd recently started a relationship with a man who'd later become my husband. I talk about how hard it was for *me*, but when I look back, it wasn't exactly Good Times for him either. I can't imagine being in a budding relationship in your midtwenties, and the first thing your girlfriend does is buy a dog, and the second thing she does is try to kill herself. It doesn't seem . . . ideal.

The first day I "checked in" (a.k.a. was admitted), I expected to see a psychiatrist straightaway. Instead, I was shown to my room and was told to rest. Fair enough. The room had a seaside-hotel vibe—a queen-size bed, a little desk with a chair, and a balcony overlooking the bay. I can't remember seeing a psychiatrist that day, but to be fair I couldn't remember much, what with all the everything.

My "outside" psychiatrist, Tim, assigned me a "companion," a person who stayed with me all day and night to make sure I didn't try to hurt myself again. Apart from the bathroom, everywhere I went, my companion came too. She was with me in my room, during meals, on smoke breaks, when I took Benny outside, and at night she sat outside my room as I slept. It wasn't the same person all the time, but it was always a woman. I know the companions were only doing their job, but I hated it. I hated being watched and followed everywhere. I couldn't have one second to myself unless I was taking a shit, and even then I knew there was someone waiting outside the door. During my short time in rehab I must have gone through five or six companions, all of whom were nice and, more important, not chatty. At that point, all I wanted to do was isolate myself. I tried talking to other patients, but it was hard. I felt like the new kid at school who always had to have a chaperone. At the time, everyone else was in there for drug and alcohol addiction; I was the only one who was there for being purely mental. It was clear the addicts were a clique. I didn't have the same "classes" as them. I attended one group AA session, and while there were some broad values I could relate to, the majority of what I heard did not apply to my situation. I kept asking to see a psychiatrist and was repeatedly told "soon" and that I should "rest in the meantime."

The lack of routine and psychiatric support, along with the abundance of downtime, was overwhelming. Three days in I was struggling. Even though I had someone with me AT ALL TIMES, I felt incredibly lonely and even more depressed. Some of you reading this may think I was an awful little ingrate, that I should have felt grateful to be in such a luxurious facility. Believe me, I was and am extremely grateful, not just for rehab, but for everyone— my psychiatrist, my dog, my husband, my dog. But here's the fun part: mental illness doesn't care how fancy your rehab is; if it feels like fucking you up, it will.

On the fourth day, I was assigned a new companion. She was different from the others, younger for one thing, maybe just a few years older than me. She was short, slim, and white. She had a messy blonde bob which, if I remember correctly, featured some faded pink and blue strands. She was dressed like all of the Alanis Morissettes in the "Ironic" video and spoke in a semihusky tone. She introduced herself as Lara*. By that time, I had a whole schtick for new companions, which went like this: "Hi, I'm Amanda," followed by silence. I gave Lara the same silent treatment and went about my day of downtime, medication, and self-imposed isolation. It was early evening, and we were both in my room. I was lying in bed, and she sat on the floor next to me writing in a notebook. I said she could use the desk, but she said she preferred the floor. I rolled my eyes, then rolled my body away from her. I heard her notebook close and was immediately like, "Jesus, here we go."

Unlike the other companions, who kept their chat gentle and mild, Lara talked to me like she was my friend. At first, I thought she was attempting a *Dangerous Minds*–type connection. I half expected her to swivel a chair around, sit on it the wrong, and be all, "Depression is whack, amirite?" But she didn't ask why I was there or what I "had"; she just talked to me about her job and everyday shit. I didn't say anything for the first fifteen minutes, because for the first time in a while, I began to decompress. I'd been so focused on not talking that I forgot how soothing it was to just listen. The combination of Lara's raspy voice and the fact that she wasn't talking about mental illness put my mind at ease. Turns out, all I needed in that moment was a chat. We chatted shit for hours—boyfriends, girlfriends, movies, TV shows, writing. I was the one who first brought up mental illness. I don't know why, but it felt natural. We'd been bitching about work or men, and I said, "You know what I hate about having a mental illness? The lack of hygiene." And instead of grimacing and asking if I was ok, she laughed and said, "Yeah, me too." And that was it. We swapped mental illness war stories into the night, much in the same way friends swap shitty relationship stories at brunch. Topics included:

▪ How you should be awarded a medal for brushing your teeth or your hair.

- How it takes days to get in the shower, but once you're in there, it takes three hours to get out.
- How wearing the same clothes (pajamas) for a week is acceptable.
- How your bed becomes a living room/kitchen/closet.

If you have a mental illness, you'll know that these aren't revolutionary observations. In fact, they're pretty banal. And that's what was so exciting! We weren't discussing harrowing trauma or stigma or grrrrr society! We were talking about depression like it was an annoying job or partner, which took away its power. By ridiculing certain aspects of our illnesses, we'd made them less intimidating.

I'm not saying that people should joke or make light of mental illness all the time (although it is what I spend most of my time doing). I'm saying it helps. I had spent so long focusing on the big, scary picture of mental illness that I'd forgotten about the painfully funny, ridiculous minutiae that come with it. It's the little things that make talking about this shit bearable. Lara didn't have bipolar like I did. We didn't share any "big" disorders, but that didn't matter because we had a ton of little things in common: isolation, putting on a brave face, shame, guilt, and constantly coming up with excuses. If you've ever felt low at any point in your life, I guarantee you'll be able to relate to someone with a mental illness, maybe not in a big way, but that's not the point. It's about finding common ground, listening, being open, and remaining nonjudgmental.

There is no "proper" way to talk about mental illness, and thank god for that! Imagine having guidelines on how to talk about your feelings. We'd all sound like dull, horny, and deeply traumatized robots, which I now realize is an accurate description of most us.

From that night with Lara, I learned that when I'm meeting someone new, starting off casually and getting comfortable with them works best for me. I don't launch into conversations with a "Hello, I'm mental!" As open as I am online about my illness, I'm not a complete sociopath. I'm able to reserve some decorum for real-life interactions. I understand that not everyone is ready to be thrown in the deep end of what it means to live with clinical depression, especially at an after-work drinks party for Karen's birthday. But if we start off small, maybe we can get to a point where no one has to announce they're mental, because it'll be a given and therefore no big deal.

That said, as with all things related to mental illness, however you choose to talk about it is the best way, just as long as you talk.

Lara left in the wee hours of the morning. She said she'd be sitting outside my room in the chair reserved for my overnight companion and she'd see me in the morning. I woke up feeling refreshed and, dare I say, excited. I couldn't wait to chat more shit with Lara. But when I opened my door, a new companion was sitting in the chair. She told me that Lara had been called away for another patient in another facility. I said, "Hi, I'm Amanda," followed by silence. Three days later, I checked myself out of the program. It wasn't working, but my conversation with Lara alone had been worth it.

You Don't Have to Be Crazy to Work Here

I don't know a single person who's comfortable telling their employer they need to take a "mental health day". But people take mental health days all the time; they just call them "food poisoning" or "appliance delivery" or "working from home." That's what we need to say because a "new fridge" is more legitimate and garners more empathy than "too depressed." I know there are some places that have policies to allow mental health days, but it's bullshit. Like "unlimited vacation," it's a trap. A company can establish all the policies they want, but at the end of the day you have to tell your BOSS that your MENTAL STATE is NOT GOOD, which is still SUPER UNCOMFORTABLE. No number of "reassuring" HR emails could convince me it was ok to tell my boss I needed a mental health day, because if there's one place that doesn't give a shit about your feelings, it's work.

I've been employed by companies big and small and have never felt comfortable telling anyone at work about my mental state. I couldn't even bring myself to tell the few bosses I liked and with whom I had good relationships. My mother's voice was stuck in my head: "This will go on your record!" The ALMIGHTY AND OMNISCIENT record I'd never seen, yet 100 percent believed in.

I used to come up with all sorts of what I call "gross physical excuses" in order to stay at home and look after my mental well-being, because "gross physical excuses" are never questioned by your manager and are the only acceptable reasons to be away from work. Here are a few samples from my personal collection:

1. "Explosive diarrhea"

It's important to use the term "explosive" because Diarrhea Classic™ just doesn't cut it. You need to make it clear that it's physically impossible for you to leave your apartment, let alone negotiate public transport. I don't know about you, but I've had explosive diarrhea before, and let me tell you, it's much easier to manage than crippling depression. But, to quote Irish icons, B*Witched, c'est la vie!

2. "Coming out of both ends"

Similar to "explosive diarrhea" but with the addition of another hole. A surefire way of securing a mental health day is by painting a vivid mental image, and nothing says "I can't come in" like "it's all coming out." Amazing how this is more dignified and socially acceptable than saying you're depressed.

3. "Fractured limb"

The low-key sister injury to a broken bone. A fracture walks the fine line between serious enough to get out of work but not so serious that you'd need to keep up the lie when you're back in the office. All you need to do is wear one of those compression-wrap bandages for a few days and you're good—a small price to pay to make sure you don't completely lose your mind!

4. "Migraine"

A migraine is more than just a headache. I've never experienced one myself, but I know many people who suffer from them, and they sound like hell. From needing to sit alone in a dark room for hours on end to vomiting from the pain, migraines do not fuck around. It's a vicious neurological disease with debilitating physical symptoms that can last for days, even weeks . . . making it an awesome excuse for when you need to take a mental health day. I want to be clear, this is in no way belittling the horror that is a migraine, we just need to use it because people understand it better than our thing. It's the holy grail: mental pain others can relate to.

5. "Family emergency"

Granted, this is neither gross nor physical, but it is effective and will never be challenged. Your manager won't (or at least shouldn't) question it, and when you return to work people will be too scared to ask you about it. A family emergency is vague, relatable, and prohibits follow-up questions—the trifecta for taking a day off so you can look after your deteriorating mental state.

It all comes back to the obvious illness versus the invisible illness: when people can *see* your suffering, they are more likely to empathize. How many times have you or someone else gone into work with a full-on cold, and a coworker is like, "You look like shit. You should go home." The answer is thousands of millions. Some people get angry and order you to go home: "You shouldn't be here! Other people could catch it!" Others take pity and beg you to "go home and get some rest." Walk into any office with a runny nose and a cough, and an angry pity mob will form as if from nowhere chanting "GO BACK HOME!" and "WE DON'T WANT YOUR GERMS HERE!" Go into that same office and say, "I feel so depressed," and you know what you'll get? "Join the club." There will be no pity, no compassion, no "take the day off." Y'know why?

Because at work, *everyone's* depressed. You're not special for feeling low at work—you're *normal*. All you need is a strong coffee, and you'll be fine.

There are several reasons why I wouldn't want to disclose my mental health at work.

Work Ethic(s)

If you're a millennial, chances are you've worked through a financial and housing collapse that you inherited and played no part in causing. You're scrambling for entry-level jobs that pay in Good Exposure, or as it's more commonly known, fuck-all, all while trying to pay off a seemingly bottomless pit of student loans. And on top of all of that, society sees millennials as whiny, spoiled teenagers when the majority of us are THIRTY YEARS OLD and FIXING YOUR WI-FI, so stop complaining. We've been conditioned to believe we are disposable and that there is a "line of people out the door" ready to take our place. And even though we're overworked into poor physical and mental health, we should feel ever so grateful we even have a job in the first place. So given that most of us are barely scraping by financially, coupled with the looming threat that we can be replaced at any second, you can see why most of us aren't willing to ask for a day off, let alone a day off for our mental health. It's not that we would rather put work before our mental well-being; it's that we have no choice. I know it sounds extreme, and I'll probably get a bunch of emails from people being all "I'm a millennial and I'm doing just fine, thank you!" In which case, godspeed with your great life and your family's generous donations. Back to everyone else—this culture of fear has forced us into deprioritizing both our mental and physical health. We are making ourselves sick in order to work longer for less. And when we're sick, we're less effective; and when we're not effective, we're replaced with a new, less sick person.

Judgment Day

When it comes to disclosing a mental illness at work, nothing is scarier than your boss's reaction and what they'll do with this new information.

I used to work in tech marketing, which meant a lot of bullshit, buzzwords, and men. Before my first suicide attempt, I worked hard to prove myself, often to the detriment of my mental health. To be clear, my job was not the reason for my psychotic break, but it didn't do anything to help. I wanted to be useful to my boss. I was fine with him taking credit for my ideas, as long as it meant I could stay on the team. I think, subconsciously, I was trying to build up some goodwill for my inevitable meltdown. I wanted to be the perfect employee, somebody reliable the team could count on. If my colleagues knew I was struggling with a mental illness, I'd be seen as unable to do the work and would be demoted or pushed out.

Employers don't have time to accommodate your mental disorders. They do, but they don't want to. There are companies that subsidize therapy sessions, which is awesome, but it doesn't take away the feeling of guilt when you need to take an hour out of your work day to go to said session. Companies can wax corporate about how much they care about their employees' well-being, but it won't matter unless they start to change the way managers think about workers' mental health. Real change does not come from HR emailing out surface-level promises; it comes from educating employees on an individual level and changing people's perception about sick and mental health days. The majority of workplaces don't even know what a mental health day is let alone the importance of being able to take one!

"But letting people take days off for their mental health will hurt the company!" says a disembodied voice I made up but which sounds a lot like Gilbert Gottfried. To which I say, "Not true, Gilbert!" If anything, employers would benefit from giving their workers mental health days because, just like with any illness, they're not going to be productive when they're sick. When an employee who's suffering mentally comes into work and feels pressured into staying, that hurt can roll into the next day and the next. They don't get a "Go home! Feel better!" They get a "Yep, it's 2019—we're all depressed."

If companies want their workers to feel mentally ok—sorry, be more efficient—then there are a few things they could start doing:

- Have a mental health professional come in to talk about mental health in the workplace on a regular basis! Not just once like, "Great we've done our mental homework for the year."
- I know this is tough for a lot of companies, but for the rich ones like in *Billions*, have an on-site counselor or therapist.
- Change the attitudes toward sick days from both the managers' side and their staff's side. For too long people have been hesitant to take sick days for fear of looking like slackers. If this doesn't change, then we'll forever be going to work sick, and that's not good for anyone.
- Allow workers to take mental health days and encourage them to take them! That's the problem with "unlimited vacation." Your boss put it on the table like, "here's all this vacation" and then lurk in the shadows, waiting, watching what you'll do with it. So you decided to take a week off. Seems reasonable, that is until the boss emerges from the dark forest like, "Oh I see, decided to take a whole week off did we? Very interesting." I'm not sure what kind of *Pan's Labyrinth* creature this boss is but my point is, taking days off is super awkward,

because even if your boss is cool with it, you still feel guilty. We need more than the boss to be "cool with it", we need them to actively support and encourage their employees to take mental health days and vacation days.

▪ This one is unrealistic, but it's the dream—everyone gets free or subsidized therapy.

Changing how people view mental health at work can help change the way we view mental health in general. There are a relatively small number of companies that actively prioritize mental well-being. If we want to see a significant shift in attitude, we're gonna need to see a lot more companies putting the work in. And this should extend beyond corporate offices; we're talking service industry, agriculture, freelancers, hospitality, retail, health care, anywhere people WORK. Now, if any company wants me to come and talk to them about mental health at work, I am very available, I am not a mental health professional, and my fee is extortionate.

The Stigma Continues

When I returned to work after my first suicide attempt, things were different from how they'd been before. A few coworkers were understanding, the rest were wary. My manager made it clear I should "take it easy for now," which is code for "I'm gonna have other people do your job instead of you." It sounded caring and understanding, but it felt like penalization for having been out for recovery. I believe I would have been better off missing work for six weeks because of a broken leg. People wouldn't have second-guessed if I could still do my job. Even when I got back into the swing of things, I could feel that coworkers were still being cautious around me. Of course, this could be my own paranoia, but from talking with others who've been in similar positions, I suspect my hunch is true.

When I returned to work after my second suicide attempt (this was at another job), my team and the HR person were very supportive. However, the boss told me that he was frustrated I had not kept them updated on my recovery. "Even a text would've been nice." I felt awful, like I'd let the team down, like I'd inconvenienced everyone with my trivial bullshit. The company was a small start-up, and people often worked through the night because, as we all know, working till the wee hours means you're a super dedicated and fully functional employee. I was never going to be one of those employees because it would kill me. I had to leave.

Trying to cover up my mental health at work became exhausting. I was leading a double life, like Clark Kent and Superman, only I was Clark Kent and Clark Kent's mentally ill twin. I found myself becoming more isolated and paranoid than usual. The last office job I had was at another start-up. The boss seemed nice at first. I knew him through mutual acquaintances, so I thought he couldn't be that bad. I was wrong. I soon learned he was a toxic, emotionally abusive bully. A couple of people left the company because of him and the effect he had on their mental health. He created a climate of fear and distrust that made it hard to talk to HR because we all knew whatever was said would ultimately get back to him. I dreaded going into work. I felt controlled by his moodiness and his mind games. The dread soon turned into depression. He'd taken such a toll on me that I finally gave up.

Maybe I'm just not cut out to work in an office. Still, no matter where you work, it seems that the stigma is always there. And I'm not just talking about the stigma around mental illness; I'm talking about the stigma of taking time off work in general! You ever get into work fifteen minutes late and some smug turd is all, "Half day?" Or you take a lunch break *not* at your desk and people look at you like you're a lady of leisure? These may be throwaway looks and remarks, but they stick with people and can be potentially damaging to one's psyche. Like many people, I've been cursed with the ability to notice and overanalyze every tiny thing—words, tones, facial expressions, all of it. So when you make a snarky comment or shoot a disparaging look, it may not be as "harmless" as you think. Many people take shit like that to heart, but people with a mental illness take it into the depths of our souls, where it lives forever in purgatory.

It's easy for companies to say they care about mental health, but it seems rather difficult for them to put that into practice. You can provide all the benefits you want, but if you don't have a culture where people feel comfortable talking about their mental health, then those who live with mental illness or struggle with their moods (so that's pretty much EVERYONE) will continue to hide, thus worsening their condition.

If you are currently employed and are struggling with your mental health, you could tell HR, sure. But not every workplace has an HR department. Even if they do, well, maybe you're scared to tell them, which is understandable. Another thing you could try is find a coworker you trust and talk to them. That way at least someone at your work knows. It's good to have an outlet at work, even if it is just one person.

If you don't want to talk to your colleagues (fair), then try focusing on what you can do for yourself throughout the day. Maybe try to carve out small pockets of time to regroup and do something that relaxes you—for example, listening to music while taking a walk around the block. Find any small activity that will help you get away from your work environment and focus on you for a bit. If all else fails and you need to go home for a mental health break, please feel free to use one of my not-so-fail-safe "gross physical excuses."

I wish I had a magic wand that turned all the workplace stigma into dust and banned coworkers from asking about "everyone's weekend plans" It's going to take a while before we see companies prioritize mental health, so the best thing we can do now (for those who feel strong enough to do so) is support each other. If someone at work confides in you about their mental illness or that they're feeling low and can't bring themselves to come into work, be there for them. If you can, cover for them. It's easy for some privileged prick to say, "If your job is making you miserable, then quit!" Don't you think we'd all do that if we didn't need money to LIVE? Just remember that taking a little bit of time for yourself for self-care is a priority. It's not an inconvenience, nor is it you just trying to "scam some time off work." It's just as important as taking time for your physical health. If you're not feeling ok mentally, then you're not going to be effective at work—simple as that. Look after yourself, not just because you should, but because your life depends on it.

What's It Like to Date a Mentally Ill Person?

I knew my husband before I was diagnosed. Before he became my friend, he was just some man at work. When we first met, he had no idea about my mental illness and neither did I. At the time we both smoked back when we were cool and carefree. I was sitting on a bench outside the office with my earphones in. I'd just lit up a cigarette when a shadowy figure entered my peripheral vision. I tensed up, as is natural for any woman who senses a nearby male, and braced myself for some sort of interaction. I heard a voice reverberate through my earphones; he was trying to make contact. I removed a single earbud, the universal gesture for "ok, but make it quick," and looked up at the offending male talker. He was tallish, well-builtish, bearded, and had brown hair and kind eyes. He seemed undeterred by the single earbud, but not in a dick way. I squinted at him, confused by his confidence and chattiness. He said his name was Pavel. I said "Cool," which stopped the conversation. I saw this as my chance; while maintaining hard eye contact, I took hold of the errant earbud and purposefully started to put it back into my ear. In a last-ditch attempt, Pavel blurted out, "I'm Bulgarian, I'm from Bulgaria . . . originally." I stared at him, half confused, half amused. There was a brief pause before he cracked a joke about work. I laughed, he smiled, and I removed the other earbud.

Pavel visited me in the psych ward during my first hospitalization. I don't remember a lot from the visits. I remember him sitting in a chair in my room and not saying much. He didn't look like his normal self (says the one who was wearing a hospital gown). Pavel is quiet and reserved, until you get to know him, and then he's still quiet but less reserved. He's naturally funny, and people often gravitate toward him at parties and dinners, which I love and am jealous of in equal measure, because I try *very* hard to be funny and charming. No one would ever describe me as "chill" or "easygoing." But when you ask my friends, they'll tell you that I'm "definitely not chill" and "honestly hard work."

Pavel was quiet in the psych ward, but it was more like a pained silence. He shifted uncomfortably in his chair and barely made eye contact. I was embarrassed. I didn't want him to see me all "mental" like this. Our friendship was built on laughter, nineties music, and chatting shit. I didn't want that to change, but judging by the way he didn't look at me, I was sure it had. This was my first mistake, and it would be a mistake I'd make over and over again throughout our relationship: I thought about how my mental state affected only me, not him.

Since that day in the psych ward, Pavel has supported me through my psychiatric hospital stay, a second suicide attempt, the subsequent rehab stint, various panic attacks, and hundreds of episodes both depressive and manic. He's not my rock; he's my motherfucking mountain. I don't want to sound dramatic (I do), but I wouldn't be here without Pavel's unwavering love and support. However, this chapter is not about how he's the best and I'm the worst, oh no. It's about how we've both been the worst and we're still trying our best.

I must admit, until I began to write this chapter, I'd never talked to Pavel about what living with me is like from his side. To be honest, I was scared. I didn't want to hear about how awful I'd made things because of my mental illness, or how he may have been tempted to leave during one of my depressive episodes, or (and this one haunted me) how he might be scared of me. Even though I'd pushed those fears to the back of my mind, they'd still come up every now and then. But now I have to write this chapter, and I can't *not* ask him!

Or can't I?

Ok no, I know, I have to ask him.

I'm gonna ask him.

Three days later.

Any minute now.

Two weeks later.

Whatever the relationship—dating, married, friends— everyone navigates the bonds in different ways. I don't know your personal situation, and thus I would never dream of telling you how to "be" with your partner or friends. The following is based on my relationship, and while some of what I write won't apply to you, I hope you'll find a few bits useful. In the short five years that Pavel and I have been together, we've experienced a wide variety of mental episodes. We had to start from scratch. No one tells you how to deal with mental illness in the context of a budding romantic relationship; you have to learn on the job. You make mistakes, then you keep making mistakes, and eventually you work it out, but then you make the same mistakes again. There's no magic solution. But after talking extensively about the impact mental illness has had on our relationship, we came to this groundbreaking conclusion: treat your relationship with your significant other like any other relationship.

I know that sounds obvious, but the most damaging situation for us was when we were both so focused on my mental illness that we didn't let the relationship breathe and grow organically. That's not to say you should ignore the illness completely, but bringing it up should be the exception and not the rule.

Here are some of the things we've learned from being in a relationship with someone with a mental illness *and* from being the person with the mental illness. In his and obviously my own words.

Early Days of Dating

PAVEL: It was frustrating at the start. It felt like playing a game you think you know the rules to, but then new rules keep getting thrown at you on the fly. The first time you see that "other side"—an anxiety attack or a hypomanic or depressive episode—it's shocking. But on the flip side, when you're in the thick of it, you can discover things about yourself that you didn't know were there. You're a lot more resilient than you thought you were. However, at the start, it felt claustrophobic. Amanda was manic a lot at the start, and I found it difficult to balance looking after her and processing my feelings. I'd never interacted with mania before, and I suddenly felt responsible for her mental well-being, which was a lot to take on in the first few weeks.

AMANDA: I'd been in an extended manic episode in the lead-up to Pavel and I getting together. I was impulsive and obsessive, and found it hard to articulate how I was feeling. When you and I first started dating, my mind was scattered like a supermarket display of fallen oranges, which exacerbated my mania. Everything was CAPS LOCK. I pinned so much on Pavel and this barely there relationship. I proposed to him in week two, he said yes, but he said yes out of fear. He didn't want to upset me. I was over the moon in a very crazy way. I went out and bought a ring for myself. Pavel soon realized how unhealthy this all was, and he told me he didn't want to get married, but he still wanted to be with me. I flew off the handle and told him to "get the fuck out of my house." When he respected my wishes, I'd break down. I continued to break up and get back together with him on a daily basis until the episode was over. Looking back, it must have been incredibly taxing for him, especially as we were only a month into the relationship by then. Most people would have thrown their hands in the air and been like, "I'm done!" Shit, I think I would have. But he never left, not once.

It's Just Like Any Other Relationship, Only Different

PAVEL: The stakes are a little higher in a relationship with a person with a mental illness, in that you could mistakenly push them over the edge by reconnecting them to trauma that you can't even imagine. You could put them in a frame of mind that's beyond your control by something you say or do. In a "non–mentally ill" relationship, you know which buttons to press with your partner to get a rise out of them. With someone who has a mental illness, everything is a potential button. It can be disconcerting at first, and you can clam up rather than risk saying anything at all. But over time you learn to think before speaking, much like you would in any relationship. That's not to say I walk around on eggshells; it's just something to be aware of. You don't need to learn a whole new skill set to be in a relationship with someone with a mental disorder. You just need to be better. It's not a stretch.

AMANDA: There were times when Pavel didn't understand why what he was saying was causing me mental anguish, which was made worse by the fact that I couldn't communicate why, either.

He'd keep asking, "What's wrong?" And all I could say was, "I don't know!" It's frustrating on both sides. He wanted specifics like "What exactly did I say that triggered this?" or "Tell me precisely how you feel right now," or "What specifically should I do to fix this?" And while I knew this was coming from a good place and that he genuinely wanted to help, all it did was stress me out. If I knew the answers to these questions, I'd never have to go to therapy again! When someone is struggling with their mental health, firing off a bunch of questions in the hope for an answer causes more harm than good. We both had these idealistic expectations of each other: Pavel would be able to pinpoint the problem, and I'd be able to deliver a solution. But nothing in life is that easy, especially when mental illness is involved. It took us a long time to understand that. It's not perfect now by any means, but when we find ourselves at an impasse, we don't focus on "fixing" it immediately. The best thing we can do is slow down, listen, and give each other time to breathe.

Upping the Empathy

PAVEL: Recognize that the other person's experience is valid even if it may be colored by mental illness. Even if something they do or say seems irrational or unreasonable, you need to accept it and learn why. I didn't learn this over time; it was just something that clicked one day.

AMANDA: When was that day?

PAVEL: Dunno.

AMANDA: Alright . . . continue.

PAVEL: Just because something is "in your head" doesn't make it any less serious. *Everything* is in our heads. Whether it's caused by their depression or not, if your partner is in pain, then they're in pain. To support them means you have to let go of the idea that there's a clear line that divides "genuine" experience and experience colored by mental illness. In the extreme, this kind of thinking can threaten your relationship. When your partner is mentally ill, it is so tempting to wave away their feedback—to invalidate their perspective in the relationship. I used this as a defense mechanism, as a way to avoid responsibility.

AMANDA: Having your friend or partner assume that the way you're behaving is purely due to your illness is one of the hardest things to stomach. It's dehumanizing; you feel less like a person and more like a science experiment. To have your feelings reduced to "that's the depression talking" not only hurts, it makes you retreat into yourself. There were times when I didn't want to share my feelings for fear they would be dismissed as part of my illness. It's shit like this that can bring a relationship to its knees. We all know that communication is important in any relationship, but when you're dealing with someone for whom talking about feelings could save their life, the stakes are a little higher. If I don't feel comfortable expressing my everyday household feelings, it hampers my ability to discuss my grim and grisly feelings, and if I can't talk about my grim and grisly feelings, my mind will try to kill me. A little extreme, but you get the gist. A good rule of thumb for anyone in a relationship with a person with a mental illness: never assume their mental state.

A Third Person in the Relationship

PAVEL: It can be difficult to tease apart your feelings about your partner as you know them versus when they're acting unlike themselves because they're suffering from an episode. This is especially hard when they want to hurt themselves; your instinct to protect the person you love goes haywire, because the person you love is also the person who wants to hurt your loved one—if that makes sense. Like, your person and your person's killer are in the same body, and they look and sound the same. It's a confusing feeling, and keeping those feelings separate is incredibly hard.

AMANDA: I can't imagine what that feels like. I've never been in a position of seeing someone I love want to hurt themselves. I don't think I've ever thought about it in-depth until now. I always assumed that this was just something a partner had to deal with, in a "take it or leave it" kind of way. I see now how selfish that is. I talk about the importance of not dismissing the feelings of a mentally ill partner, while all this time I'd been dismissing Pavel's feelings. I made it so that I could be the *only* depressed one in the relationship or the *only* one who could have anxiety or be stressed. I had the monopoly on all things mental. On the outside I'd preach about how "everyone's experience is valid" and "we should listen when someone reaches out," but in my own relationship, I did the opposite. Every time Pavel showed the smallest sign of mental struggle, I'd hoist myself up on my high horse and be all, "Try being bipolar, then talk to me." There's no excuse for that behavior. It's certainly not caused by mental illness; it's simply being a hypocritical dickhead. I'm embarrassed at how long it took me to come to terms with all of this. I can't and won't apologize for having a mental illness, but I am sorry for taking my partner for granted and for not recognizing how it can affect him. I, too, have had to increase my empathy and understanding, because no one *owns* mental illness. We all lease it.

Talking to Others

PAVEL: If no one else knows about your partner's mental illness, you can't talk about it with your friends, and you don't *want* to talk about it either. Are you really gonna be that person who complains about their partner's mental illness? It seems weak and unfair. I find it hard to talk to anyone about my feelings. Funnily enough, I'm better now *because* of our relationship. It's improved my communication skills, increased my capacity for compassion, and made me a better person in general. That said, I still don't air these grievances with friends. How do you tell someone you're scared of your girlfriend?

AMANDA: You're scared of me?

PAVEL: I was. Not anymore.

AMANDA: Damn, ok . . .

At first, I felt more comfortable talking about my mental illness online than I did with Pavel or my friends. For the most part, I could keep internet strangers at arm's length, thus avoiding any meaningful interactions. I could have my one-way cake and eat it! I became reliant on blogging about my feelings (which helped!) rather than talking about them. I was in therapy at the time, which led me to believe I had the best of both worlds—I talked to a human twice a week, and the rest of the time I talked into the ether. Luckily, a few friends saw and connected with my online ramblings, and they reached out. Some were good friends, others just acquaintances. Either way, it felt good to have an honest dialogue with someone who wasn't my psychiatrist. Once I opened up, it became easier to reach out to real-life humans. People assumed that just because I wrote so candidly about my illness online that I was the same way offline, and that couldn't be further from the truth.

Medication

PAVEL: There's no good way to ask your partner if they've taken their medication. It'll always sound accusatory. I used to dole out Amanda's medication, but that ended up annoying her.

AMANDA: Yes, it felt like he was my nurse, but not in a hot way. Sometimes in a hot way.

PAVEL: I now just have an alarm set for "medication time." It's a good way of reminding Amanda about her meds without seeming like I'm on her case about it.

AMANDA: I know that the fact that Pavel sets an alarm must sound like he's a weird control freak, but you must understand that I have a history of going off my medication without warning, so this system works for us.

Anything Else?

PAVEL: Just because you're good at taking care of someone in a crisis doesn't mean you get credit to allow you to neglect the rest of your relationship on a day-to-day basis. Your partner's experience is valid all the time. Also, I recommended seeing a therapist for yourself if you can. You're going to see and experience some shit that isn't exactly typical of a "regular" relationship. It can be traumatizing to see the person you love want to hurt themselves, and it's good to be able to unpack that with a mental health professional. It'll help you process and be prepared for the next time.

The best advice I could give is to just be there for your person. Don't try and be their therapist, because you'll probably do more harm than good. Talk through issues. Figure out what worked and what didn't work. You won't be great at the start, but use these opportunities to learn because there will always be a next time.

AMANDA: The most important lesson I've learned is that I'm not the only one who's allowed to feel depressed or anxious. In the same way that I don't want my feelings dismissed, I shouldn't dismiss others' either. Just because you don't have a diagnosed mental illness doesn't mean you don't hurt or suffer. Just because your friends and partner are there for you during your dark times doesn't mean they're not affected too. I took that for granted for a long time. So yeah, just keep talking and listening and learning. Honestly, it's like any relationship, only mental.

PAVEL: We good?

AMANDA: We're good.

Love in the Time of Wanting to Kill Yourself

I didn't grow up in a demonstrably lovey-dovey family. We didn't really hug or kiss or say things like "I love you." I don't mean this in a "Boo hoo, I was so unloved!" kind of way. I'm sure there was love there; it was just unhealthy and super conditional.

That's what gets me about love: the word itself is often associated with warmth and joy.

"All you need is love." NOPE. You need a hell of a lot more than love, like food and shelter and Wi-Fi.

"Love like you've never been hurt." Great advice if you like getting hurt a lot.

"If you love what you do, you'll never work a day in your life." You will absolutely work most days of your life.

"Love is the answer." It's not.

Love is generally meant to be a good thing. Even when it comes to heartbreak, the reason why it hurts so bad is because, at one time, the love felt so good. (Side note: am I a country singer/songwriter now?)

I want to talk about a different strain of love, an unromantic love born of toxic pools of delusion and control.

Being raised by or being in a relationship with a narcissist means you exist purely for them. You become an empty vessel for them to control, fill, and empty, whenever they so wish. These twisted dynamics warp your entire notion of love. You see love both as a weapon and as life support. You're constantly on edge because you know this "love" can be ripped away at any time. But, more importantly, you don't feel worthy of love, so you begin to hate yourself.

For over twenty years I nurtured that self-hate. I let it cloud my thinking. I actively sought out relationships with narcissists. The "love" they gave was the only love I knew, and although it was killing me, it felt safe. Toxic love felt like home. Sound familiar? These types of relationships are super common. You don't have to be raised by a narcissist to feel undeserving of love; it can happen to anyone. I was programmed to feel that way from a young age, so when my mental illness surfaced, I felt that much more of a burden to my family and friends. My depression and mood disorder exacerbated the hatred I felt for myself, creating the perfect conditions to grow suicidal thoughts. I craved "love" from men who hated me, so much so that it sent me flying into bouts of mania.

My first suicide attempt occurred in the middle of a perfect shitstorm. My mental health had taken a nosedive, and I was spending all my energy trying to hide my mania and depression, both of which seemed to come and go as often as labor contractions. I was in a relationship with a man who was at best, ambivalent toward me, and at worst, hated me. I didn't love him, but I loved that he hated me. As I circled the drain, all I could think about was how much I deserved this. I was so ensconced in my own self-loathing that even an ounce of love felt alien and strangely hurtful.

I became wary of love. I assumed there was a catch when anyone showed me the slightest bit of kindness. My concept of what it meant to love and be loved was much like a Magic Eye image—distorted and something only other people experience, and dolphins, it's always dolphins. For me, love was neither plea-sure nor pain; love was a plague. And if you felt love, either from yourself or others, then you deserved to be punished, and not in a sexy way.

It took me years to learn how to accept love, and it's taking me a lot longer to learn how to love myself. Shit, I'm thirty-two goddamn years old, and I still struggle with *liking* myself. I have, however, managed not to hate myself so much. So how did I do it? Great question! It's taken years of hard work in therapy to get to this point. Here are a few things I learned that helped me not hate myself:

1. Cut out toxic people.

Easier said than done, I know! Especially when you're related to them. I'm not suggesting you just quit people cold turkey (although if you can, that's cool too). I'd start by weaning yourself off them at a steady pace. Toxic people are super demanding of your time; they need you on call at all hours. And yet, when you need them, they're weirdly unavailable. Try to limit contact, and learn how to say no. Saying no is a beautiful thing, and I wish I'd learned how to do it sooner. Saying no to other people is saying yes to yourself.

2. Do something for you.

When you've spent most of your life being told you're not good enough, you believe it. As a result you stop doing stuff you want to do. You avoid trying new things or taking up hobbies because what's the point? You're gonna suck at it anyway. And I'm here to tell you, DON'T BELIEVE THAT SHIT. I took up writing "prop-erly" in 2013, after I was discharged from the hospital. I decided to do something for me, and it didn't matter if I sucked at it or not, because this was mine, and no one could take it away from me. I realized I didn't need to be "good enough" to love myself. I first needed to learn who I was: my likes, my dislikes, whether I was one of those people who used the word *epic* (I'm not). For the record, I didn't "date" myself or try to "find" myself in another country. I just picked something I'd always wanted to do and did it. I'd been in a holding pattern for so long that it felt good to finally land.

3. Reframe and confront the voice in your head.

The aftereffects of narcissism are long-lasting. To this day, I'm unable to completely block out the voice in my head that says, "You're bad." Ok, granted it's not a super articulate voice, but it's hurtful nonetheless! I've been fortunate enough to have enjoyed a little success in my life, and at every point I've heard an inner voice say, "You don't deserve this." This is not uncommon, especially among people who are not straight, white, and male. I don't have a great solution for combating these feelings other than to simply sit with them, which is hard, because they're scary. Anytime I sensed that voice speaking up, I'd run as fast as I could. I didn't want to hear or be near it. But the more I ran, the louder it grew. By the time it caught up to me, it sounded like a foghorn in my ear. I decided to stop running, to confront the voice and talk to it. I know this sounds mental, but it works—not all the time, but sometimes, and sometimes is better than no times. I listen to the voice with a different mind-set from the one I had before, and when it talks, I pity it. I hear its desperate attempts to break me down, to reassert control. And the fact that I can recognize all of this proves the voice wrong. Sometimes it helps to sit with your pain rather than bat it away. And although it's terrifying to confront such trauma, doing so will ultimately make you stronger for next time, because there's always a next time.

I know it sounds bleak, but I don't think there will ever be a day where I don't hear a voice reverberating in my head, telling me I'm "not enough." Which is ok, because I know I'm well on my way to liking myself, and soon that loud, brash voice will trail off into a whisper. Love is not all you need, but loving yourself is a start.

PART 6
Not Ok but Ok

A Meeting with My Mental Illness

In Attendance:

- Depression
- Anxiety
- PTSD
- Amanda
- Bipolar

(Amanda, Depression, Bipolar, and PTSD are seated. Anxiety is standing, facing the wall.)

Amanda: Thank you all for coming.

Depression: Eh.

Bipolar: No.

PTSD: The last time we were in this room, it was a complete nightmare.

Anxiety: *Muffled speech.*

Amanda: We've been working together for . . . how long is it now? Ten years? Give or take. And it's clear that our processes are a little chaotic. With that said, what I'd like to work on in this meeting is a streamlined system whereby we can all work together seamlessly and thus—

Depression: I'm out.

Bipolar: If Depression is out, then I'm out.

(Anxiety turns to face the group.)

Anxiety: DON'T LOOK AT ME.

(Anxiety turns back to the wall.)

Amanda: Listen, everybody's work is overlapping, and we're not getting anything done. It's a mess.

Bipolar: You're a mess.

Amanda: See? We're not leaving this room till we've come up with a solu—

Bipolar: I'm in.

Amanda: Yeah? Ok, nice. Who else? Depression?

Depression: On one condition.

Amanda: Yes?

Depression: I don't do anything.

Amanda: That's literally . . . ugh . . . How is that being *in*?

Depression: Wow. Puh-ret-tay judgy for someone with so many illnesses.

PTSD: Hey now! She's like this only because of all the death she experienced growing up. Remember all the death, Amanda?

Amanda: Yes, thank you, I—

Anxiety: (*Whispering.*) I think the best thing for us to do is just leave and never speak to each other again.

Bipolar: SPEAK UP. WE CAN'T FUCKING HEAR YOU!

Anxiety: (*Whispering.*) I think the best thing for us to do is—

Bipolar: SHUT UP. WE HATE YOU.

Anxiety: (*Whispering to self.*) I knew it.

PTSD: (*Tearing up.*) You were just sixteen years old when he died.

Amanda: Ok. So I've come up with a schedule where everyone has an individual slot.

    8:00 a.m.–2:00 p.m.: PTSD
    2:00 p.m.–9:00 p.m.: Depression
    9:00 p.m.–8:00 a.m.: Anxiety
    And, I guess, Bipolar can pop in and out whenever.

(*Bipolar does the gun-and-wink gesture at Amanda.*)

Depression: This makes no sense. The morning slot is where I shine, everybody knows that! And also the evening . . . and early to late afternoon.

Amanda: I want to make sure everyone has their own time because it'll make it easier for me to manage the workload.

(*Anxiety sits down in one of the chairs.*)

Anxiety: Do you really think it's best for *me* to take *evenings*? I mean, isn't that when you go out and socialize?

(Everybody laughs heartily for ten minutes.)

Amanda: *(Wipes away tears of mirth.)* Ok settle down, settle down. I've put forward my plan. Does anybody else have any suggestions?

(PTSD raises hand.)

Amanda: Any suggestions that do not involve reliving traumatic memories?

(PTSD lowers hand.)

(Depression raises hand.)

Amanda: Any suggestions that do not involve killing myself?

(Depression keeps hand raised.)

Amanda: Ok, D. But you have to promise you won't tell me to kill myself.

Depression: I promise. This is a really good suggestion.

Amanda: Well then, I'm—

Depression: Kill yourself.

Amanda: Cool. Anyone else?

Anxiety: I mean, I have suggestions. But why would you want them from me? Who am I to give suggestions? People hate my suggestions. People hate me. Including the people I'm close to. Maybe not . . . Maybe you don't hate me. Maybe I'm just imagining things, overthinking it. Yeah maybe I'm overthi—

Depression: We all hate you.

Anxiety: You see, and I *knew* that.

Depression: May I suggest—

Amanda: Don't—

Depression: Killing yourself?

Amanda: Goddammit.

Anxiety: Oh man, Depression is so much better at this stuff than I am.

Amanda: No! Listen—

PTSD: Amanda, remember when *you* tried to kill yourself?

Amanda: Yes, thank you. Now can we please get back—

PTSD: I'm talking about the *second* attempt, not the first.

Bipolar: NOW WE'RE HAVING FUN.

Anxiety: This is giving me anxiety.

Bipolar: WHO'S UP FOR A GAME OF BOGGLE?

Amanda: Shut up! Everyone just . . . just shut up. It's clear we're not getting anywhere, so we're gonna have to reschedule.

Anxiety: Yeah, I can't make the next meeting.

Amanda: I didn't say when it's going to be.

Anxiety: I can't make whenever that is.

Amanda: In the meantime, you all can go back to doing whatever you were doing because, honestly, what's the point?

Depression: That's the spirit!

Bipolar: Don't listen to them, Amanda. You can do this! I believe in you!

Amanda: You're right. I can do this!

Bipolar: Yeah! YOU'RE THE BEST!

Amanda: I don't know if I'm the best . . .

Bipolar: LET'S WRITE A SCREENPLAY REAL QUICK. IT'S ABOUT A GIRL WHO LOOKS FOR LOVE IN ALL THE WRONG PLACES BUT SHE'S A GHOST AND SHE LOVES TO FU—

Amanda: Fuck it. Everyone get back to work.

(Anxiety leaves. PTSD leaves. Bipolar leaves.)

Depression: Hey listen, I'm sorry about what happened just now. I want you to know, from now on, I'm going to try and do better. I promise.

Amanda: Hey, thank you. Genuinely. That means a lot coming from—

Depression: Kill yourself.

Amanda: Ok . . . hahahaha, you got me! Got me again with the ol' kill-yourself gag. Nice, nice.

(Depression leaves.)

(Amanda stays in the room and sings "Landslide" quietly to herself before noticing the transcriber is still here.)

Amanda: What the fuck? How long have you been—

END OF TRANSCRIPT

Small Things I Do
When I Want to Die

Thoughts are horrible. I hate having thoughts. They're quick, chaotic, and painful, like a thousand pissed off wasps trapped in your head. Even good thoughts hurt, as my mind always finds a way of turning them bad. Now, before you suggest meditation to me, I'm warning you: don't. If meditation works for you, then you can skip this chapter; this one is for the people who have an adverse reaction to silent contemplation. Yes, I have tried mindfullness, and yes, I have attended a workshop, and yes, my therapist gave me some "tips" on how to "clear my mind," but it doesn't work for me. Whenever I try to "clear my mind," you know what happens? THOUGHTS. Anytime I carve out a little bit of space for clarity and peace, that's when the angry wasps come swarming in. And because I'm in a quiet place (a key requirement of meditation), the thoughts are that much louder and harder to ignore. It's the same thought-inducing environment as bedtime, which, as we all know, is peak thought rush hour. Again, if the "decluttering" and the "deep breathing" and the "imagine nothingness" work for you, then awesome—and, also, why are you still reading? I told you to skip this one. I, on the other hand, need a distraction, especially when the thoughts go from bad to dangerous, which they often do.

Depressing thoughts are awful and stifling, but they can some-times be managed. People can go a whole day carrying depressive thoughts in their head; they can go to work, see friends, maybe even go out, all while managing a stream of anxious musings. But as soon as these thoughts begin to spiral and morph into suicidal ideation, that's when shit becomes unmanageable. Suicidal thoughts are all-consuming. If depressing thoughts are cold and gloomy, like a fog, suicidal thoughts are toxic and humid, like a gas. Fog may cloud your thinking, but gas will debilitate you. I've been up against suicidal ideation more times than I care to count, and there's no amount of meditation that can diffuse it. When I'm contemplating ending my life, I don't need another way to *think*; I need something to *do*.

One of the key ingredients in the suicidal thought process is the feeling of hopelessness. You see yourself as a burden who offers zero value to your own or anyone else's life. First of all, FALSE. You are absolutely NOT a burden. You offer a ton of value, and I'm going to prove it.

A few years ago, I came up with a list of small things I can *do* to stave off intrusive, harmful thoughts. There are strict requirements these small things must meet:

1. **Simple**—super straightforward to carry out
2. **Universal**—can be done regardless of financial status
3. **Short**—should not take up too much time
4. **Easy to accomplish**—highly doable, thus building a sense of achievement

If you're able to do *one* thing from the list below, then you add value.

Make your bed.

Assuming you make it out of bed. No need to go overboard, but maybe think about straightening up the duvet and pillows. It'll make you feel a little grown-up and will definitely add some class to your midafternoon depression nap.

Write one email.

Any email, any length. It can be to a friend, to a work associate, or to yourself. And don't feel the need to send it. The simple act of executing something start to finish will help you feel like you've achieved. Who knows, maybe you'll write another!

Reply to one email.

Similar to the above, but this time, send it. Again, don't put too much pressure on yourself. Replying to people you haven't gotten back to in weeks can be daunting, but boy does it feel good getting that weight off your shoulders.

Go outside for at least one minute.

You can walk around your block or just up and down your street. Just get some outside air and move your body a little. If it feels ok, do another minute. Keep going until it doesn't feel good.

Read the first chapter of a book.

You know that pile of new books on your bedside table? The ones you put there because you've convinced yourself you'll read them one day? The ones you sometimes put out to impress a date? Yeah, those ones. Why not pick up one of those decorative puppies and have a go at the first chapter. If you're into it, keep going; if not, stop. Easy.

Clean house for at least one minute.

This may be one of the harder tasks on the list, but, for me, doing household chores can be pretty therapeutic. I enjoy the repetition and how it keeps my mind occupied. There's no room to think of anything other than "I'm cleaning right now." It's the perfect task for those who don't like meditation; it delivers the same results *and* you have clean spoons again! Accomplishing a household chore or two gives you a sense of pride; you're caring for your home and by proxy, for yourself. It also gives you a sense of continuity; you're prepping for the next hour, day, or week. This type of "grounding" activity forces you to think ahead, which is so important for when you feel like taking your life.

Take a shower.

It takes me around three hours to get into the shower, but once I'm there, I'm there for another three hours. It's a jam-packed day of fun. Seriously, there's nothing better than showering, and I'm not just talking about getting clean. Everything (apart from sex) is better in the shower. Crying, singing, masturbating, fake arguments, acceptance speeches—ALL BETTER IN THE SHOWER. And although getting out of the shower is a pain, once you're out, you'll feel a whole lot better, because you can get right back into bed.

Talk to yourself in a different accent.

Why not? There's no one around. Just don't do a racist accent. Although I am always offended by people's fake British accents, like how are "Mary Poppins" and "Guy Ritchie movie" the only two you all seem to pick from? If you're going to mock our accent at least have the range.

Stretch.

Doesn't have to be a full downward-facing dog or anything like that;

any old stretch will do. Stretch your arms to the sky, shake your legs out, get the blood moving. It's a small task, but it'll remind you that you're alive, and that's the point.

Cry.

If you're not crying right now, and if you feel comfortable in your surroundings, go on, have a good cry. You may be thinking, "But I don't have a reason to cry," and I'm here to tell you, you don't need one! There's always a reason to cry—look at the world we live in. Also, crying makes it easier to get to sleep. It feels so good to tucker yourself out with tears and then doze off into a early-evening depression nap.

Scream.

Similar to crying only less wet.

Do a jigsaw puzzle.

I spent most of my free time in the psychiatric hospital doing jigsaw puzzles. I became addicted to the peace it brought me. Much like cleaning house, the puzzle took up all the space in my brain. From finding the piece, to finding the hole, to putting the piece in the hole (yes, I know how this sounds and I don't care), every step in the process made me feel good. Every time I matched a piece with a hole, it gave me an overwhelming sense of accomplishment. I felt like I was adding value, like I was working toward something bigger, like a Still Life, a Parisian Street, or an Underwater Scene. I spent hours sitting in the communal area with a thousand puzzle pieces strewn across the table. Other patients would come up and take a look, and soon a few joined in. We'd start off silently searching and placing pieces in our respective "corners," but soon we became a team, a SEAL Team Six of jigsaw puzzle solvers. One of us would man the picture on the box, directing the team to the correct area, while another would compile the edge pieces, making sure they were all in place before we attacked the middle. Something as simple and analog as a jigsaw puzzle made us feel less like individual mental patients and more like teammates. When you feel like part of a fun and supportive team, it makes you feel less like killing yourself.

Write a letter (to anyone) on paper with a pen.

I say "letter" but it can be anything. Draw a picture, write a bullet journal—anything that requires pen and paper. If anything, you'll think, "Damn, when was the last time I actually *wrote* anything?" Then you'll at your wildly illegible handwriting and think about how much importance they placed on handwriting at school. Then you'll be like, lol remember school? And you'll go down that weird rabbit hole which is better than thinking about that other thing.

Lip-synch a revenge love song in the mirror, and pretend your ex is in the audience.

Self-explanatory. Can be paired with Cry and/or Scream.

Fold your clothes.

If you're depressed, chances are your laundry (both clean and dirty) is in a pile on your bed. I know you like having it there—it's convenient, you're depressed, and you like reshaping the pile into that of a human body whom you call Raphael. I GET IT. That said, if you can, try repurposing your laundry lover into folded piles of clothes. It's another repetitive task that'll keep you somewhat sane, and at the end of it you'll have more space in your bed for that late evening depression nap!

Reorganize your desktop.

Everyone's laptop is a nightmare—random folders, photos, and documents plastered everywhere. It looks like the celebration sequence when you win solitaire, but instead of cards, it's files. Every now and then I try to delete and consolidate these files (a.k.a. empty drafts). I don't do it to be organized, although that is a bonus by-product. I do it because deleting feels so fucking good. It makes you feel powerful and in control. Have you ever selected two or more folders and just hit "delete," like a GOD? Maybe it's just me, as I don't have a lot going on. But there's something so satisfying about destroying old crap on your laptop, and don't get me started on emptying the trash. If you have a Mac, you'll understand what I mean when I say that the sound that plays when you hit "empty trash" is orgasmic (again, I do not have a lot going on). When it comes down to it, it's the little things—especially the ones that make you feel in control—that help fight suicidal ideation.

Exist.

This is the hardest one. But if you can do any of the above, that means you're existing. And simply by existing, you're adding value. There are many different versions of lists like this one. You can find them on the internet. If my list or other people's lists don't work for you, that's ok. Make your own. There's no wrong way to make a list of things that will help you. Whatever you do—whether you scream, cry, or jerk off in the shower (or all three at once)—just stay with us. We're lucky to have you.

Being Ok in the Grey

I have always been a stubborn, argumentative butthead. Even from a young age, I'd find it hard to back down from a good (nonphysical) fight. So it shouldn't surprise you that I was one of those insufferable debate kids. At my school, debate wasn't as big as it is in the US. There were three people on the "Pro" side, three people on the "Con," and one chairperson. It took place in our small school gym, and all the students would cram in to watch. This was my sport.

It wasn't hard to get on the debate team. All you had to do was present a few salient arguments to the teacher, who'd shrug and be like, "Ok, cool." When I was thirteen, my debate teacher asked me why I wanted to be on the Pro side of the issue of animal rights. I don't remember the specifics, but I'm pretty sure it was about whether animals should have rights or not, real nuanced stuff. Anyway, I went on this huge rant, making my overly earnest points and using unnecessary hand gestures to demonstrate said points. I didn't debate so much as present a closing statement in a high-profile murder trial. I looked the teacher smugly in the eye as if to say, "Case closed, bitch." He nodded and in an exasperated tone said, "Yes, Amanda, you're on the team." I think I did a small bow because, as mentioned previously, I was an insufferable child. I turned away triumphantly.

"But . . ." he said.

My head spun round like an angry owl.

"You must debate for the Con side."

I couldn't believe it. How very dare he! Of course, I tried to argue my way out of it, but the teacher insisted. He said I needed to see things from a "different perspective," which I already did—I thought he was nice, now I saw him as a dick. I eventually agreed to argue for Con and ended up losing the debate.

These days I'm lot more rational but still just as annoying. Even so, when I'm in the depths of my mental illness, it feels like that time in debate all over again. Whether it's depression, anxiety, or whatever mood my bipolar decides to plunge me into, my entire sense of perspective goes out the window. I've been in situations where my mind point-blank refuses to see anything other than darkness and despair. If I'm depressed, I will never *not* be depressed again. If I have anxiety, I will never be calm. If someone gives me constructive criticism on my writing, it means I'm the worst writer and must never write words ever again, and also that person HATES ME. I'm sure a lot of writers feel this way, especially those that aren't straight, white, and male. People doubt themselves all the time. We walk around acting humanesque on the outside while living like an imposter monster on the inside—VERY NORMAL. It's easy to fall into self-doubt, but with a mental illness it's near impossible to climb out.

I envy people who are able to "take a step back" and assess a situation. Honestly, what is your life? Are you also able to "let shit go" and "not worry about it"? Because if you are, then (1) fuck you and (2) teach me your ways, how I long to be chill! To be fair, I know people like this. I married someone like this, and I'm still in awe of how they exist. It must be all that extra rest they get from not having to overanalyze. Every. Single. Thing. My. God. I, on the other hand, live in a world littered with grudges, pride, and ego.

It's not a popular opinion, but having a mental illness can make you self-centered and childish. When you're wading through a mire of depression and someone glides in all "Maybe we should paint the bathroom blue instead of green?" And even though it's a good suggestion, all you hear is "I'm challenging you in this, your time of need. How dare I?"

There have been plenty of times in my work, marriage, and friendships where my judgment has been skewed due to selfish shortsightedness. I become the only person in the world suffering from depression, and everyone else just doesn't understand me! *Slams door, plays angry music.*

I'm the only one in my relationship who's allowed to shout and cry.

I'm the only friend who's allowed to cancel plans.

I'm the only coworker who's allowed to eat the leftover cake in the fridge from Karen's going-away party because I'm depressed AND I DON'T KNOW WHY YOU'RE PISSED OFF THIS CAKE ISN'T VERY GOOD ANWYAY.

Bathroom colors and cake aside, there's a dangerous side to this type of black-and-white thinking, because once those blinkers are on, they ain't coming off for a while. You're stuck in either extreme black or extreme white, both of which are restrictive and exhausting. It's like being trapped in a prism devoid of context or reasoning; it's just you and your one view infinitely reflected back at you. There's no compromise, there's no empathy, there's no grey.

A harmless comment can send you into a tailspin; it can seriously affect your relationships and your work and can drag you deeper into depression. The same goes for being in limbo. I've found that something as harmless as waiting on a reply from someone can set me off into a maelstrom of lunacy. If someone doesn't get back to me within twenty-four hours, my mind concocts an elaborate stage play of what could be happening on the other end, complete with musical numbers and intervals. I'll fixate over every interaction and fantasize about the worst possible outcomes. I'll confide in my therapist about these ephemeral obsessions, to which she replies with the most unhelpful sentence known to man, "Just wait and see." ARRGGHHHHHHHH! WAIT and SEE? Those are literally THE TWO THINGS I WILL NEVER DO. I'd rather her say, "They haven't got back to you? Wow, they must really hate you" Because at least it's something I can grip onto.

It's not easy to "take a step back" when you have a mood disorder and are currently in the throes of having a singular point of view. It's as corny and unrealistic as telling someone to "snap out of" their depression or "stop looking at your phone at night if you want to get to sleep."

To the "mentally well" otherwise known as "liars", this may be another thing that sounds super dramatic and completely controllable, and I wish you were right. Believe me, I wish I could take several steps back. I wish every new thought didn't crash into my chest cavity like a spaceship re-entering the earth's atmosphere. I wish I could silence my thoughts by plucking them out of the ground like flowers. I wish my thoughts could let me breathe. But they can't and I can't. The one thing I can do, is S L O W I T T H E F U C K D O W N. Like Neo slowing down bullets in *The Matrix*, only the bullets are thoughts and I'm married to Keanu Reeves. Or like in *John Wick* only the bad guys are thoughts, I'm still married to Keanu Reeves, and the puppy survives. This is my book, which means I get to write whatever I want, and I say the puppy LIVES.

Anyway, back to mental illness.

Most people understand the term "grey area" as an ill-defined situation or field. There are people who use it to excuse racism, abuse, sexism, and rape. Let's be clear: NONE OF THOSE THINGS HAVE A GREY AREA. They are ALL HORRIFIC AND WRONG. The grey I'm referring to is more of a halfway house for intrusive thoughts—a place that allows you to temporarily examine and potentially manage any guilt, judgment, or fury before spinning out of control. But the grey is hard to find; the roads leading to it are long, winding, and often veer off a cliff edge. Once you reach the grey, the first thing you notice is that it doesn't look like the pictures on the website. You thought you'd be luxuriating in one of those fancy Big Sur Inns, but instead you're at Motel 9 (or is it 6?) on the outskirts of Reno. The grey does not have the answers. The grey is a rain check. It will not bring you peace or clarity, but it can postpone your spiraling, and sometimes that's all you need.

When I feel a possible trigger hurtling toward me, I try to do something completely unrelated to that situation, like a load of laundry. And before you jump in with "This sounds like avoidance," let me tell you something: it absolutely is avoidance. There's no way your mind will let the entire thing slide. But by sidestepping it, even for a moment, you can dampen the initial sting. You don't need to feel good in the grey; you just need to tolerate it. And isn't that what life is all about, folks? Tolerating shit until you die.

I don't want to end a chapter on the phrase "tolerating shit until you die," so I'll leave you with this: When your mind is susceptible to depression, sudden mood changes, PTSD, or any mental disorder, every interaction is a potential minefield and every thought can feel like a battle. Our minds are anything but weak; they're fucking jacked! Do you know how much strength it takes to fight an infinite invisible army? I don't know the exact unit of strength, but it's A LOT. There's no shame in sitting out a few rounds. "If I stop fighting, I'll die!" Not true. It's not all about fighting. We don't have to attack and resolve everything straightaway. We can give ourselves a break, a brief time-out to get as much shit together as we can, and then we can carry on. I may never feel good again, and I'm fine with that, as long as I can be ok.

Whatever Gets You Through This Life

Ah, the last chapter. This is where I tell you how, despite all the trials and tribulations of having a mental illness, I've "come out the other side." This is where I tell you how much I've "changed as a person," and how you, too, can be like me: enlightened, hard-working, and healed.

But you already know that's not happening.

It's ten in the morning on a chilly summer day in San Francisco. I'm writing to you from my bed because I'm in the middle of a brutal depressive episode, and because this where I write. It's taken me a little over a year to write this book. In that time, I've experienced multiple manic episodes, extended periods of depression, suicidal ideation, and inescapable anxiety—all the classic emotions when writing a book. I JOKE. But seriously, I wrote a few chapters while manic, I'm sure you can tell which ones. This is my normal, this is SO MANY people's normal, but out there (I'm pointing at my window) we're still treated like feral babies who desperately need everyone's zesty takes on mental illness.

We don't.

We're tired.

Take your takes elsewhere. Better yet, take 'em to a therapist.

In the past few months, I've attempted to re-connect with my parents. It's been traumatic to say the least, but both have been receptive. We're far from being a happy family, I mean, you could hardly call us a family let alone happy, but you can call us related people who talk now, and that's good enough.

Why would I reach out after all these years? Well, I believe there are only two things that could bring an estranged family together and those are death and/or birth. In my case it was the latter.

. . .

. . .

Wow yes, thank you for noticing that I did indeed write this WHOLE ASS BOOK while PREGNANT. I, too, question the whereabouts of my Medal of Freedom/National Book Award. Anyway, thank you for your ongoing support of me winning awards, it truly is the only reason I write.

Anyway, back to this, the dreaded last chapter. I feel like you're all watching me, waiting for me to say something meaningful and advocate-y. ARGH DON'T LOOK AT ME. I'm sorry but I really don't know what I'm doing. My body is made up of 80% imposter and 20% petty grudges from nine years ago. Part of it is just being a woman, but mental illness can also make you feel like a fraud. It can make you question everything from your entire existence to your ability to navigate a supermarket. Making you feel less than is one of mental illness's key value propositions. It sells "Because you're not worth it." And we eat that shit up. Mental illness is a real, serious business, like Apple, only the product is an elaborate scam, like Apple, but we continue to buy into it because, y'know . . . Apple. We have no choice (she writes, on her Macbook).

We never *chose* to have a mental disorder—the same way people don't *choose* to have diarrhea (unless they choose Chipotle). It's also not our fault. We spend a lot of time hating ourselves and blaming ourselves. We internalize so much guilt and shame that it fuses into our bloodstream.

I spent so much time worrying about how my mental illness affected my friends, family, and general standing in society that I forgot about me. I put all my effort into shielding other people from my crazy; I'd left no shelter for myself. It's taken me years to learn that my mental illness is my own, which means I have to do whatever works for me and me alone. No one has your same mind or body; therefore, no one can possibly know what you're going through. That's not to say we shouldn't listen to anyone else's stories—quite the contrary! Sharing and listening to other people's experiences is one of the ways we drain the shame from mental illness. And by "other people's experiences" I mean EVERYONE, especially those whose stories often don't make "the front page." A key part to tearing down the stigma is to start listening to and highlighting stories from marginalized groups: Black women, trans women, Black trans women, Asian women, all people of color, the LGBTQ+ community. Sharing, listening, and believing these stories can make people feel heard, understood, and valid. Most importantly, we want to make sure people don't feel alone, especially those most at risk for suicide like our queer and trans youth.

Don't worry, straight men, I haven't forgotten about you. Go to therapy.

Do not pass go. Do not collect $200. Go to therapy.

Whether you think you need it or not, go to therapy, because you absolutely need it. If you're infuriated by this suggestion and feel like you want to send me an indignant rambling email or a boring sweary DM, then by all means, prove me right harder.

Talking about your feelings is not as easy. And before I go any further, I want to apologize for the following sentences. I honestly did not mean for them to sound weirdly sexual.

Talking about your feelings is not as easy. It's not something that comes naturally and it's not something you can force. It takes time and practice. It may not feel good while you're doing it, especially the first time, but I promise you'll feel relief afterwards. If you don't feel ready to talk to someone else, maybe talk to yourself. Seriously, as long as you let it out, you'll feel better.

I still find it challenging telling my closest friends how I feel, so much so, that they're going to read this book and be like, "YOU WHAT?"

The way I reconcile sharing feelings is by thinking of it like a jigsaw puzzle (I know, I'm obsessed). When you first buy a puzzle, all the pieces are wrapped in a plastic bag, and that bag sits in a box, much like your thoughts and feelings. If you were to leave the pieces in the bag in the box, they would sit there and rot. Ok, maybe not rot, but they wouldn't be used to their full potential. Every time you talk about how you're feeling, you're taking a piece of the puzzle out of the bag and putting it on the table. If you're able to see a therapist or a counselor, the pieces come out quicker. Before you know it, all the pieces are laid out and facing up. Now you need to put them together, and how you do that is up to you. Some people start with the edges. Some start from the inside and work their way out. Others like to study the picture on the box first. We all have different ways of putting the pieces together, and it doesn't matter which way or what pace we choose, as long as we're doing it. That's all that matters. It may take you a week, a month, or even a year to connect two pieces, and that's ok. Unlike sports or *Bachelor In Paradise*, there's no set of rules or carefully crafted script for how to get your mental shit together (although, if someone could come up with those, that'd be GREAT). As long as you're not hurting yourself or others, do whatever works for you. Whatever gets you through this life.

There's no shame in having a mental illness, or going to therapy, or taking meds. And while it feels like most people know this already, I only have to travel back six years or so when I felt deeply ashamed of my mental state. Six years is not that long ago (although these days every hour feels like a millennia) but six years ago I felt more alone than I've ever felt in my life. I felt like a psychotic monster, a terrible daughter, and a failed human being. Which proves there must still be people who *don't* know there's no shame in having a mental illness. And if you're one of those people then you're in luck because I wrote this book for you. I wrote this book for people who suspect they have a mental illness. I wrote this book for those who are struggling with it. I wrote this book for people who have accepted it. I wrote this book for everyone, because everyone is mental.

And I wrote this book for Amanda from six years ago, because I'm pretty sure she'd need it right now.

Here I am, six years later. I've learned a lot and grown a little. I'm not happy but I'm ok and that's good enough for me. Because that's all we can really hope for—being good enough for *ourselves*.

APPENDIX

MENTAL HEALTH ORGANIZATIONS

content TK

ACKNOWLEDGMENTS

content TK

CPSIA information can be obtained
at www.ICGtesting.com
Printed in the USA
LVHW092144030519
616649LV00001B/2/P

* C S 0 0 0 0 5 9 3 9 J R N *